thrive

how HIV changed everything

Copyright © 2025

Thrive Publishing

All rights reserved.

ISBN: 9798274830829

intro

Why, hello there. If you've picked up or downloaded my book, you might be thinking a few different things right now. Either you thought you were picking up a self-help book about how to beat burnout, balance life, or just lean into self-care. Maybe you saw a cute twink, and thought, hmm, where did he get that hat? The topic of HIV might have piqued your interest.

While all of those might be true, you might also want to know a little about me and what brought me to writing this book. Thrive is the combination of all three of my previous memoirs to connect the dots and offer the most complete version of my story to date. It will also discuss my experience with HIV, and how it truly changed my life.

My first memoir, "Running Home" was published during a time of intense desire to prove myself and my worth in a space that was unwelcoming of my identity as a gay man. The first book was so cringy that I unpublished it several years ago after writing my second memoir, "Walking Forward". While "Walking Forward" referenced the first book a little, it never really told the full story of what happened before the second book. While there are bits and pieces sprinkled in, I wanted to offer you a clearer picture of my life and what happened to me through a raw, non-religious, non-testimony, lens.

My third memoir, "Own It" was once the pinnacle of my story where I recounted a bit of my story along with my experience surrounding my HIV diagnosis and later local activism and research. While I only touched on my diagnosis in "Own It" a bit, I thought that allowing myself space to reflect on the impact it had on my life would be a useful tool, not only for myself, but for those who might see a reflection of themselves in my story. Regardless of why you picked up my book, and what you expected to read here, I'm so grateful that you did.

Before you begin, I want to provide a warning for anyone who has experienced childhood trauma, suicidal thoughts or ideation, emotional and physical abuse, domestic violence, or discrimination because of your identity or illness. The elements in this book are heavy in nature and can be triggering to some. Take care of yourself while reading and if you find yourself in a personal mental health crisis, please dial 988 for immediate assistance.

I also recommend having the tissues handy as I talk about a lot of personal traumas that might be sad or disturbing to some. I'll tell you now, there is a happy ending if you can just hold on to the end. Like everything in life, it does get better.

one

Life… where do we even begin, you know? What is the meaning of our everyday lives? How do we live in a world so mundane, so ordinary? Is it ordinary, or is it something extraordinary we have yet to discover? Can we find happiness amid our sufferings? Can we allow ourselves to enjoy our lives under the weight of life's circumstances?

My life began, like any other life, at a hospital. A place where people who are suffering come for healing. People who have physical ailments, mental challenges, and even the common cold come to be cared for and nurtured by nurses and doctors. It seems ironic to me how our lives begin in a place that is surrounded by pain and suffering, yet, we begin with eyes wide open to things we have yet to discover.

Growing up, my life was like any other young boy's life in Northeast Arkansas. I lived in Hoxie, a town snuffled right next to a slightly bigger town named Walnut Ridge. It's funny thinking about it today, it seems so long ago. The two towns absolutely hated each other though the names of both towns were plastered on the same sign as you entered the area. Walnut Ridge was the bigger of the two with a population totaling around 4,500.

Then there's Hoxie, the abandoned train epicenter of the area with a population of 2,000 or so. Don't get me wrong, we still had plenty of trains, but they never stopped there. They just blew their horns at midnight every weekday to wake up the entire town as they passed through.

Our house was a humble abode, a fixer upper if you will. There were lots of things wrong with it. The roof leaked; the floor was wavy because the foundation wasn't stable. The ceiling over my bed even had a hole in it covered by a thin piece of plywood. A piece of plywood so thin that you could hear the cats that would often reside in our attic. It was a good home for a while though. To me, it represented my dad's desire to provide for his family.

When we moved into our house, I remember a large pile of sheetrock in the living room, countless cans of dark green and light blue paint, and construction that seemed to be happening all the time. If it wasn't one project it was another, but my father's sincere desire to provide a life for us was profound and something I still think about a lot.

When I was in second grade, my sister was in tenth. We rode the same bus to school, and we would often have awesome conversations, sometimes funny and sometimes serious. It was on those bus rides that we really began to grow our relationship. Sometimes I look back on those days. I remember those times with a lot of joy and comfort. My seven-year-old heart was beginning to know what it means to love.

As life moved on in those early years of my life, I began to discover what it means to love people despite the differences each represented. Today, I am still learning what it means to truly love someone.

At a young age, I realized I was quite different from my peers. I felt things a lot more deeply than others, started to show more and more sensitivity, and would quickly realize that not everyone loved church as much as I did. It wouldn't be until later that I'd discover why. In Sunday school we would always be pressured to "witness" to someone each week and report back the following week with how it went. I took it seriously and would always try to "witness" to my classmates in my group. Some would flat out tell me to stop talking to them and others were a bit more receptive. At seven years old, I just thought I was doing the right thing.

At this young, easily influenced age, I thought church was the coolest place ever. It was the first place that I made friends, met elderly people, and heard about a higher being that somehow took the time to love me too. We went to a small church that was just down the road from our house. Starting with just a couple Sundays a month, we eventually called that church home for many years. It was there that I discovered friendship, compassion, the importance of giving, and many other principles that a "good person" should possess. It's also the place where I, without fully knowing what I was doing, gave my "heart to the lord". Church slowly took over my young life and I wouldn't realize until much later the pain and torment that it would end up causing to my mental and even physical health.

While there are many reasons why I look back on my time in the church with a lot of regret and pain, there are a few things I am thankful for. Church was where my love for music began and grew. When I was ten, shortly after my parents got divorced, I started to play piano. At first, I would tinker around the little keyboard that my sister had bought for piano lessons. Of course, she didn't like that I wanted to play it too. It was mostly because I was horrible at it. The only song that I knew how to play was Chopsticks, which was the song that my grandma had taught me. As I began to play more often, I started to try other things. I would try pressing one key instead of another. I would play some black keys with the white ones to see how they might sound together. Music became a lifeline for me, a momentary escape from the trauma I was experiencing.

As I grew just a bit older, I began to learn and play special songs at church. They were all worship songs with a maximum of four chords that were easy to learn and even memorize. As I practiced more and more, I began to develop a passion for playing the piano and I even began to sing. I didn't know how I was learning so fast. I could literally hear a song on the radio and have the entire thing down in thirty minutes. Maybe it had something to do with that four chord thing.

Shortly after my parents got divorced, we started attending another church about thirty minutes from our house. After the divorce, my dad had become a zombie. I was so sad to see how depressed he was. Before the divorce, he seemed so full of life, and so happy. Looking back on the time when my parents were still married, I should've seen it coming. My mother and sister would fight constantly, leaving my dad in the middle to be the mediator, while I watched on the sidelines, taking notes of what not to do to piss anyone off.

They would fight over the smallest of things. Screaming, yelling, and slammed doors would be the end of most nights at home. My father was the only one holding the family together, and he was struggling at that. He seemed clueless as to what to do about all the fighting. If he sided with mom, sis would get upset. If he sided with sis, mom would threaten to leave. The months leading up to the divorce were hard, and the months after were even harder.

I didn't see it coming. No one did. One night, my mom left the house on foot. While I still do not understand the entirety of what happened, what I gathered later is that my mom threatened my dad in the middle of the night and later decided to leave. I was "shielded" and "protected" from what happened by my sister and father, but I was a smart kid and knew something wasn't right.

My tenth birthday came and things started to change. I will never forget my birthday 'party' at the local Pizza Hut. I was so excited to have a birthday cake with a classic car on it, but I noticed something. My mom wasn't there. My father and sister were, all upbeat and happy like they were trying to hide something or distract me from the reality of what was going on.

My mom was in the mental hospital. At the age of, now, ten, I didn't understand. I remember going to the hospital and not being able to see my mom for some reason. She would send gifts with my dad, but I didn't understand why she couldn't give them to me herself. Then, my mom went on "vacation". The conversation went something like this.

"Why isn't mommy here?"
"She's going away for a while. She'll be back just to see you, okay?"
"But…I want to go with her! I don't understand!"
"She'll be back, okay? Don't worry."

I remember a specific visit to the mental health facility when my father, sister, and I all went to visit her. She was in a facility in the closest town over and my dad had tried so hard to allow me to see her. I remember frustrated conversations at nurse's stations, hushed looks of aggression, and visitation hours that turned into quick glances at my mom through the glass on the second floor, from the parking lot.

She never came back, not permanently at least. Once she got out of the hospital, every other week, I would get to see her. My mom and dad weren't holding hands anymore, weren't even looking at each other. They would sit at opposite ends of the room from each other. I guessed mom was still on "vacation".

A couple years passed, and I slowly lost my relationship with my mom. It was just my dad and I. During this time, I felt like I was hanging out with my best friend, but at the same time, I also felt like my best friend was a zombie. My dad would talk to me, but he was so distant at the same time. Looking back, I think my dad had a deep case of depression.

Life without mom and my sister (after she went to college) was hard. Our family didn't enjoy things like we did before. Christmas trees were just painful to decorate. A stark reminder of a life that was once very happy and warm, now cold and stagnant like a bitter December night. Thanksgiving dinners were minimal and out of a box. It was weird and incredibly sad.

My dad was struggling to find work after the shoe factory in our small town laid everyone off and closed. To try to bounce back, my father enrolled in an IT program at the local college. One of the fun things about having a parent in college was getting to go to class with him. I 'learned' so much about physical and computer science that I really didn't know what to do with it. I was only about twelve or thirteen at the time, but I took notes just like the rest of them. I felt so 'grown up' walking into class with my dad. He even gave me a notebook so that I could take notes on what the professor was teaching that day.

After the divorce was final and mom was permanently "on vacation", things started to change. The "every two weeks" visitations allowed me to learn that my mom had left my dad for a woman. Overnight, I went from the cool, normal, kid at school to the kid whose mom is a lesbian. Everyone knew and treated me differently because of it. It was a small, conservative town, and word, especially something this controversial, traveled fast. I was mortified. I had no control over my social situation as the bullying began. In addition to being made fun of for how skinny I was, I was now the skinny, gay kid. I remember the desperation in my heart as I tried everything to prove that I was not gay. This began my desperate attempts to prove to everyone that I was not my mom.

No one believed me as I drifted away from my once close friends. I wasn't cool anymore and I could not do anything to change it. As the bullying got worse, I poured myself into my studies. I wanted to be good at something to at least feel like I belonged somewhere and that my contributions were valued. As the years progressed, I tried several times to prove I was not who everyone thought I was. Several allowances spent on flowers, cards, and jewelry ended up in trash cans around the school. I felt trapped in a world I did not choose.

My teetering social life was mirrored by the house I grew up in. The floor was not even, there were holes in the walls, and mold grew all over everything. It wasn't great and I remember having an internal longing for something to bring light to my life.

During this turbulent time, I found comfort in attending church and allowing myself to think that there was a God who loved me and could do something about what I was facing. It was at that same time that I started to believe that I was who everyone thought

I was. I would hear message upon message shaming homosexuality, demonizing it, and presenting it as a conscious choice that someone would make like the type of soda they drink. I wanted to scream, "I didn't choose this!", but no one would listen and my hatred of myself would only grow deeper. Confused and discouraged, I could not bear to think that I was such a horrible person that pastors made me out to be. I was a loving person that just wanted to feel like I belonged somewhere. I was attracted to other guys. I didn't understand why, but I knew what and how I felt.

    I continued to try to prove that I was not who everyone said I was, but the task seemed impossible. When I tried to be one of the boys, I was rejected and labeled as weak. From about ten years old on, I was bullied and found reprieve in pouring myself into my schoolwork, hoping to make something of myself. There were several teachers that I owe the world to who helped me get through this time. Although they didn't know the internal struggle that I endured, their support and belief in me was profound and has shaped me in ways I'm still reflecting on and discovering. It would take a while to mention each one by name, but if you're one of those teachers reading this, thank you from the bottom of my heart.

Early on in my childhood, there were two librarians that really changed my life, allowing me to be one of the library helpers. This was a special opportunity as it allowed me to learn how to shelve books and know all there was to know about how a library operates. My later years of school would be speckled with more teachers that helped me gain confidence in myself again and help me believe that I belonged and was worth more than I thought I was.

two

Growing up, after school was a stark contrast to the joy and fulfillment I found in my studies. After having a wonderful day wrapped up in the wonderful world of knowledge, I would wait outside the school for my dad to pick me up. I would see parent after parent pick up their kids from school, smiling and seeming happy to see them. The crowd of kids would get thinner and thinner as I waited for my dad. 3:30pm would come, then 4:00pm, then 4:30pm, then 5:00pm. Multiple days I would have to act like my dad was picking me up at the community center just across the school campus. I would act like my dad had picked me up so the teachers could leave. There was an afterschool program, but my dad couldn't afford to pay for it.

You could see the highway from the community center, and I remember watching all the cars pass, wondering why it was taking my dad so long to get there. As the minutes got longer, I started losing hope that he was coming at all. On cold days, I would stay inside until it got too late for me to, and the teachers and administrators would go home. Then I would use my backpack to cover myself for warmth. On hot days, I would try to stay in the shade to stay cool. Then, I would finally see his car and get so excited to see him. I would get in the car excited and was met with a dad who seemed distant, disconnected and stressed most of the time. My excitement quickly faded as we went home.

I have a love hate relationship with this part of my life. In some ways it was wonderful. I enjoyed the time that I had when it was just my father and I, even though, at times, he was distant and seemed distracted and uninterested. During this time, something happened at the church we were attending in our hometown and we left and started attending a church about twenty minutes away from our home. I wasn't quite sure what it was, but I think it had something to do with my father's divorce.

The new church was about 30 minutes away from our house. Every Sunday and Wednesday, we would go and afterwards, we would go to Waffle House and have dinner. That is where we met someone who would become a great friend to the two of us. She was a sweet, older lady that was so kind to us and even had our order memorized after just a few visits. She was excellent at her job and would almost have our order ready shortly after we sat down, every single time we stopped in.

As our relationship with her grew Sunday after Sunday and Wednesday after Wednesday, she would allow me to clean her tables for her and give me some of her tips. All these years later (as I am writing this) I'm sitting in the same Waffle House I came to with my dad. I come to this Waffle House a lot to remember my dad and the good times we had together. I guess I keep coming hoping that he might walk through the door. He hasn't yet and he probably never will. He has a new family now and has left my sister and I behind. I still cling to hope that one day he will realize what he did to us, what he did to me.

As the months progressed, my dad became the soundman at the church we were attending. I enjoyed being the sound-man's son, especially when he allowed me to help. I slowly learned how to play piano with the help of several people at church. I could not read sheet music, but I could play chords and learned a lot of the worship songs that we would normally sing at church. I became confident in my ability to perform and started entering in various contests sponsored by the church. I won several awards for it, and it gave me a sense of accomplishment and helped me get through that part of my life.

One Sunday, after a change in leadership at the church, the pastor pulled me aside and asked if I would want to lead worship. I was quite nervous, but I said yes and became the interim worship leader. I learned all kinds of worship songs, most by listening to them over and over and picking them up rather quickly. I poured myself into it and enjoyed it a lot. I would lead worship every time the doors were open. I would practice at church for hours on Sundays to make sure I could keep time and have a good sound. I had some timing issues, but everyone was incredibly supportive of me and seemed to be able to connect to God through the music I played.

I led worship for several months until the church leadership found a new worship leader that was qualified and more experienced. This was hard for me because when they came in, I was taken off the platform completely and led worship for my small teen class on Wednesday nights. I tried to understand why and it was difficult, but eventually I got over it and moved on. During this time, I entered in the talent exposition hosted by the church and won several awards that I still have and hold dear.

My dad was so supportive of my musical talents, so much so that he helped me produce my very first album, "He Is Jesus". I wrote all the music on the album, and we would record it using the sound system at the church. We did several recording sessions on Sunday afternoons, and he designed the cover and everything. I was a bit of an entrepreneur back then and had a small box that I sold my CD's out of. Everyone seemed to like my music, and I was so happy they did. I had one small issue though. I hated to listen to myself. I sold one to my social studies teacher and she played it for the class. I was so embarrassed to listen to myself that I had to go out in the hall while she played it. I did end up making some money from my music and really enjoyed the feeling of accomplishment I felt doing it, but my inner saboteur couldn't cope.

Life felt good when it was just my dad and me. As life moved on, it was obvious that things were changing. My dad would smile at me, but when he would look away, a look of sorrow would wash over his face. I could tell he was lonely, and I knew that he was not completely happy with the way his life had turned out. I could tell he was trying, but I know he was trying to be strong for me after everything that happened. The days after the divorce were very complicated. My dad was putting himself through school in his early 40s, and it was not a good financial situation for the two of us. Some nights all that we would have to eat would be canned Pork 'N Beans. Among other cheap things, Ramen Noodles were most of our meals. When we did eat out, my father would also scold me and make sure I ordered "something you'll eat!". He was trying hard to take care of me, but maybe just a little aggressive with how he did it.

    It broke my heart to see my father this way. He was trying so hard to keep it together. He tried not to show his pain, but there would be nights, after I was supposed to be in bed, that I would listen at his bedroom door as he cried himself to sleep. The sobs would quietly cut through the air as I'd grab my teddy bear and try to get some sleep.

    Watching my father try so hard to

provide for me and better himself through education was inspiring. I often think about those days, drawing parallels to where I am now in my life. I see myself in the father I once knew, hoping that somehow, somewhere, he might know that I looked up to him, even when he was struggling.

three

In the months surrounding my parent's separation, I remember visiting the new library that had just opened in the next town over. Moving from its long-standing previous location, the new location was complete with a snack/coffee bar and about triple the amount of space from the quaint building it once inhabited. Part of the opening of the new location included a book/magazine sale where you could find all kinds of things. I remember being so excited about it because I wanted to grow my personal library that I had worked so hard to build. Inspired by my work as a library worker, I put little stickers on all my books with a "barcode" drawn on with magic marker. This was the perfect opportunity to add to my 'home library'.

Looking through the magazines, I remember coming across a Motor Trend magazine. With a cherry red corvette on the cover, it was a man's magazine filled with ads for auto parts stores, beer, and even the occasional Viagra ad. While flipping through the magazine, I stumbled across an article about breast cancer in men. While I had little interest in the article, what stood out (and aroused) me was the close-up of a shirtless man's chest, chiseled and tight like any random muscly guy you might see at a gym. I remember being instantly impacted by it, feeling a tingle in a place I hadn't before. After getting a good 30-45 second look at it, my father's voice cut through the air. "Son, you ready?"

"Can I get this!?" I replied, showing him the cover with the Corvette.

"Yes." He responded with a proud half-smile on his face.

My dad tried to date. Oh man, he tried. After graduating with a degree in Computer Science, he finally landed a job working for a school district. While he was there, he met someone, an elementary teacher who would constantly 'need assistance' in her classroom to fix something she had, no doubt, broken herself just to see him. It was a little awkward when we went over to her house. I would play HotWheels and Bakugon with her son while she and my dad would talk. It was kind of fun at first. She was sweet, made us dinner a few times, but she wasn't the one.

Then, my dad met my, soon to be, stepmom. My dad and I made an avid habit of eating at the local KFC. I really didn't understand why we had to always go to KFC. It was subtle at first, but it slowly turned into four, five, and six times a week. I just thought my dad liked the food, but it turns out, that's not the only thing he liked. She worked for KFC at the time and made the absolute best KFC Famous Bowls. After trying various things on the menu, I pretty much stuck with the Famous Bowls, but only got one when she was working because she would put extra chicken in my bowl.

Then, on one visit, I noticed that my dad started looking at her like he used to look at my mom. I was a little bit confused, but I tried to accept it. It was hard because I didn't really contact my mom much. Not that my dad didn't let me, but I got to the point where I really didn't want to. So much had changed, I didn't even know what we would talk about. I was alienated from her.

A couple months down the road, my dad popped the question. I was surprised, but happy to see him in a non-zombie state. We had a family wedding at a small community church that we went to occasionally. Life was starting to change. I went from being the only child to being the oldest of six with number 7 coming a year later. It was an unexpected adjustment for sure.

four

The storm came quickly like wind before a hurricane. Slowly, my stepmom started to verbally abuse me. She would yell at me because I wasn't doing the chores right. Not that I did it on purpose, but my parents never really taught me how to clean. It was just my dad and I for such a long time that we didn't care very much how the house looked. At first, I dealt with her criticism and passed it off like she just didn't understand me. I tried to make these moments a way that we could bond, and she could just teach me how she wanted things, but she would get so frustrated and toss dishes in the soapy water so violently that it scared me. I wouldn't do something right and she would get mad instead of trying to patiently teach me the right way to do it. Most of the time it was frustrating because I had no clue how to clean and she was SafeServ Certified.

Then, my father and stepmother discovered I was gay. I remember the night like it was yesterday. I was in my room and was browsing the internet looking at attractive guys on the iPod touch I bought with the money I made from selling my CDs out of the little box

I made. He barged in my room, and I jumped a bit when he came in. He grabbed my iPod and looked through it. After scrolling through the google image results of "hot gay men", he gave me a look of disgust, ran out of my room, and went downstairs to talk with my stepmom.

I had a full-on panic attack as I waited to see what would happen next. I remember staring down at my hands and watching them as they shook violently. My dad and stepmom were anything but accepting and my father made me watch as he smashed the iPod touch into bits on the concrete outside the back door. His anger and aggression toward the iPod scared me, thinking that if he were that violent toward the iPod, how would he treat me?

To alienate me even more, the broken iPod was placed in a Ziploc bag and hung on a hook over the kitchen sink, reminding me, every time I did my daily chores, how much they hated me. Then came the impossible list of chores that plagued me as I was unable to enjoy any part of my life. After school, it was homework, chores, dinner, and more chores. They took everything away from me and piled on the chores to a point where the only break I had was at school. I remember having to mop the floor with only a rag and a bucket of soapy water. I felt like a slave and trapped in a life that I could not get out of. Their demands were relentless and to this day I still have to push away their voices when I clean my own home. I must constantly tell myself that I deserve a nice, clean place to live to get it done.

The verbal assaults went on for a long time. Our house became full of unhealthy tension. My stepmom and I would have good patches from time to time, but no matter how hard both of us tried, we just couldn't get along. We tried, oh we tried, but nothing worked. We stopped going to church shortly after the wedding which was something I didn't like at the time. She always made it a fight about choosing God over her or choosing me over her or choosing literally anything else over her. The list of chores got longer and longer. The demands became more and more as the list of things I was grounded from got longer and longer. The pseudo-happy family we started with slowly dwindled away into a tension struck mess.

On April 20th, 2012, I ran away from home. My stepmom had my stepbrother, and I clean the kitchen after returning home from an all-day drive to pick up the other four kids my stepmother had partial custody of. Before marrying my father, my stepmother had several marriages with children that she now had either full or partial custody of. We would see 'the other four' as we called it, for short, every other weekend as schedules allowed. The visits were often uncontrolled chaos that struck our already tense situation. Like a tornado hitting a small hurricane, the 'other four' would descend on our house and help us forget for a weekend how much we hated each other.

    This chilly April evening, we all piled out of the suburban at around 1am after being on the road for most of the day. We survived the several hour trip to the northeast corner of the state to pick up 'the other four'. These weekends were often an attempt to entertain them more than anything else and help my stepmom feel more connected to them.

    When we all got inside the house, my stepmom had my

stepbrother and I clean the kitchen. As I was sweeping the floor, my stepmom came into the kitchen. Apparently, I missed a spot on the floor. Covered by a pile of laundry, the spot was in the small laundry room just off the kitchen by the back door. She saw that I didn't move the laundry and completely lost it. She started yelling at me, and I tried to explain how tired I was from the ride and that I didn't mean to miss a spot, I just didn't think to move the laundry and sweep underneath. She was furious and after having a big

blowup argument, she told me to go for a walk. So, I did.

Tears streaming down my face, I walked along the side of the highway at 1 o'clock in the morning. It was April, so the air had a slight chill, but luckily, I grabbed my jacket before I left. I didn't know what to do. I was crying so much I could barely see the dimly lit road in front of me. I had become a slave in my own home with no outlet to enjoy my life. At this point, they had taken everything that brought me joy. It's like they were just looking for reasons to take things away from me. First, it was the Nintendo DS for a tiny spec on one plate. Then it was the PlayStation 2 for the fingerprint they found on the fridge door. Then, I couldn't even see the TV because I missed a spot on the counter. It was a fresh hell where my only escape was school. I had to get out, and this was my chance.

    Bright lights came around the bend as I wandered through the night. As the car passed, I hoped that it wasn't a cop or anyone that I knew because I really didn't feel like explaining the situation. Then I heard the car slow down and make a U-turn. I have never been so afraid in my life. Then I heard a familiar voice cut through the midnight air. It was one of my classmates, a super butch guy that sometimes joked about copying my answers in biology class. As he pulled up slowly behind me, I tried to compose myself. I had snot running down past my lips and was sweating profusely. The composure I tried to muster, vanished as soon as I tried to answer him. In between sobs, I told him what had happened through the rolled down car window. He asked if he could give me a ride and I told him I had no clue where to go. I've never felt so alone in my life.

As I climbed into the car, he explained that he didn't have room for me to stay at his house. He was hosting a party or something and he didn't think it was the right vibe for me at the moment. I didn't know where to go. The only person I could think of was a friend I had made when I first started at the new school. She invited me to sit with her group at lunch one day and I ended up sitting with them every day after that. There was something about her that just allowed us to click. I couldn't pinpoint it at the time, but years later, she came out as lesbian and is now married to her best friend. I guess I unconsciously, even deep in the closet, I knew my people and gravitated toward them.

I had never been to her house, but he had. He knew where she lived and took me there at, now, 2am. I didn't know what to think as I awkwardly knocked on her door.
"What if she doesn't answer?"
"What if she does…with a gun?!"
"What if her mom answers and starts yelling at me too?"

After about fifteen or twenty minutes

of knocking and ringing the doorbell with headlights shining behind me, her mom answered the door. I apologized profusely as I attempted to explain the situation, now crying once again. She was so gracious, woke my friend up, and invited me in. As I sat on her couch, the world seemed to spin around me.

"What just happened?"

"Am I homeless now?"

"Where do I go next?"

I was confused and frustrated to say the least.

She asked me about what happened, and I explained the situation for the third time now. As anyone on the other side of my situation might react, she didn't know what to say. She was comforting and listened which was really all I could ask for.

I ended up staying the weekend with my friend. The next morning, she had to take her dog to the vet to get its nails clipped. As you might imagine, this was a very painful process for the dog, but perhaps more painful for my friend as she watched on as the vet clipped her whimpering dogs' nails. I tried to reciprocate the care and consideration she had shown me just a few hours before, offering words of comfort and support. The rest of the weekend was uneventful. I remember sitting on her front porch, eating pizza and staring out into the woods, wondering what direction my life would take next. I had a weird peace about leaving home, like I had tasted fresh air for the very first time. Home came with tension, frustration, and an overall sense of dread that I just didn't feel like I belonged anywhere. It was weird feeling more at home at a friend's house than my own.

  Monday morning came bright and

early. As we jumped into my friends restored vintage mustang, I became more and more anxious. The thought of my father showing up with the entire police department and possibly the Air Force was something that felt like a real possibility in that moment. I really didn't know what to expect as we pulled into the school parking lot. I remember sitting in the passenger seat a little longer after the engine clicked off, looking over at Ashley as the nerves started to set in.

Most mornings, I'd walk into school from the bus, having listened to music on my iPod on the way in. It was the one thing they hadn't taken away from me yet. Maybe it was because it was so small that they didn't realize I still had it. I don't know, but either way, I was happy that I still had something that helped me forget the hell I experienced at home. I'd often stare out the window, looking for something that could bring me hope. The beauty of nature or a bluebird, or even the childlike joy that came from drawing on dew covered windows in the heart of winter. Just anything to keep me going.

 Normally, I was the quiet, reserved kid who sat alone at lunch or with a group of loose acquaintances. Now, I was the kid who ran away from home over the weekend. As I walked in, everything seemed normal. It was a small town, but it didn't seem like everyone knew yet. As I entered my first block class, I didn't know how to look my classmates. I remember sitting down in my assigned seat as I tried not to make eye contact with anyone. It was English class, and I tried to focus on our "bell ringer" but all I could seem to accomplish was writing my name in the top right corner with the shakiest penmanship I had ever written. I couldn't even bring my hand to cooperate to write the date. 4/23/2012 just wouldn't come.

I was desperately trying to focus on the bell ringer, a quick, five-minute assignment that started every class. As I tried to focus on editing this sentence full of misspellings and misuse of grammar, I was jolted by a loud announcement coming over the intercom.

"John Caldwell, please come to the office. John Caldwell to the office. Thank you."

I was still shaking with anxiety as I gathered my things and slowly walked toward the office. As I walked into the counselor's office, I witnessed my dad putting on the act of "Father of the Year" with the counselor. I bit my tongue as my father put on the act:

"I really don't know what happened!"
"He just left; we've been worried sick!"
"I promise I will keep him under control."

He acted as if I was a monster, or a pet dog. I bit my tongue until we were escorted into a conference room to "resolve our issues". Then, I spewed. I told my dad that I was done acting as a slave and I was done living in such a stressful situation. He brushed it off like I was the one being unreasonable. In this moment I remember being struck with how different he had become. He was so cold and careless and had no regard for how I felt.

In tears, I followed him out to his car. I went to his work for the rest of the day. I didn't know what to say to him to make him see what I was feeling so I just remained quiet.

Apparently, he already had a plan because when we got home, we quickly switched from his classic Oldsmobile to the Suburban that could carry all of us. My stepmom had already packed all my clothes while I was at work with my dad. We started driving and no one would tell me where we were going. I remember a hundred different things racing through my head in that moment.

"Where are these monsters taking me?"
"What if they just drop me off in the middle of nowhere?"
"What if it was military school?"

I slowly figured out that we were going to my grandfather's house. He lived about three hours away in the same town as my uncle. When we arrived at my grandfather's, he was already asleep and didn't come to the door. I guess he didn't know we were coming or had expected us to arrive earlier. After waiting a bit, we went to my uncle's house just a few minutes away. My father was on the phone with him in the car, explaining how he needed help and how I was the reason everything was going wrong in his life. He just needed to get rid of me.

    When we went inside, my uncle showed me the room I'd be staying in, giving me a small tour of the house. After seeing my room, I just went in and sat on the bed. I didn't want to come back down to face my father.

    This had happened once before. They would think I was being unreasonable or didn't clean something properly on purpose and would pack me up and threaten to ship me to my uncle's house. Anywhere had to be better than the hell I was living in. My father would threaten to leave by walking out and closing the door, just to reappear five minutes later. It was like he was trying to re-traumatize me over and over to the point where I was completely numb. At this point, my heart had grown so cold that I didn't care if he left. Didn't care if he ran off the road into a ditch or a meteor shower took him out. If he wanted to pawn me off on another family member like I was a piece of trash to be thrown away, I wasn't stopping him. I was beyond finished with the shit they put me through.

    I stayed the next couple of months with my uncle part time and my grandparents the other part of the time. I finished my sophomore year at the nearby high school, this being high school number three. It felt like an opportunity to start again. New people who didn't know what I was going through. A fresh start.

One of my fondest memories of attending this school was going to an awesome concert with the band. I was still playing alto-saxophone at this point and was able to use a loaner instrument after my dad and stepmom sold mine to pay for something. When I came to the new school, I was able to be a part of the band and choir and even got to go to a Dallas Brass Concert. My grandparents had paid for the ticket and really just wanted me to have a good time. I did, and I remember being happy for the first time in a very, very long time.

As the school year came to a close, I found a volunteer job at the local salvage yard where my uncle worked. I have to say, I didn't think working in a salvage yard would be so enjoyable. It was awesome! I didn't do too much because of liability issues, but occasionally, they would have me pick up tires around the yard on a four-wheeler and have me clean up the shop. When it got too hot, I'd come inside and help Mrs. Betty pack shipping orders with shredded paper and bubble wrap. It was really one of the best summers of my childhood and I'm grateful for all the memories I have because of the time I spent with my grandparents and extended family.

 I remember very fondly when I won several academic awards at the end of the school year. My father mailed them to my grandpa's house, and we spent an evening handmaking frames from the scraps of wood he had in his shed. It was one of the many memories we made together in their little single wide trailer. It was obvious that my grandparents truly cared about me from the very beginning. They gave me space to process things and would sometimes even wake me up with a fresh cup of coffee on my bedside table.

That summer, I also got really close with the neighbor across the street. The sweetest, older widow you've ever met, she would let me help her water her incredibly beautiful garden and would even cook for me sometimes. I remember a shepherd's pie she made for me one afternoon that I still think about today. It was so delicious and I wish I had the recipe to recreate it now. That summer was a summer of healing and I'm so thankful for all the wonderful people who gave me a soft place to land and reflect.

As the summer came to an end, my heart was starting to change a bit about my situation. I had this swirling thought in my head, wondering if my dad and stepmom still cared about me. I would think about all the other students at school who had wonderful families and how I could be missing out on having the same thing. With all the evidence to the contrary, I weirdly felt guilt about the whole thing and thought I could be the better person and try to mend things. I didn't know if they even wanted me at this point. Everything I had experienced until that point had told me they didn't, but I was young and stupid and hopeful for a family, so I finally called my father.

  It was mid-July, right around his payday which was the 20th of every month. I dialed the number, and as soon as he answered you could feel the ice between us. I told him about how things were going, and he seemed irritated that I was doing so well. At one point, he asked to talk to my grandfather because he felt like they weren't doing enough to 'punish' me. What he didn't realize was that the real punishment was all the abuse I endured while living with him and his monster of a new wife.

Throughout our entire conversation, he seemed so distant, like he was putting on an act to make it seem like he cared about me. I knew the truth, but it was hard for me to let go of the dad I once knew before he got remarried. I had a glimmer of hope that the father I knew before still existed and hoped to finally find him again.

In the days after the phone call, I began packing my things and preparing myself for what was next. Looking back, I don't understand why I really went back to them. I guess I longed for them to love me the way I attempted to love them, but it was a hopeless endeavor I still regret today.

five

I went back home…worried, scared, and at a loss as to what was going to happen. The ride was quiet and awkward. I didn't know what to say. I felt like a stranger they had picked up on the side of the road. I thought about trying to break the ice, but, instead, I said nothing. The silence was unbearable. I was so worried that they were going to do something to me that I just sat there completely silent. I stared out the window of the suburban like I had all those times before on the bus, desperately looking for a glimmer of hope, something that I could hold onto to keep me going.

At first everything seemed to be going okay. I tried to do everything they told me to, and as I did so, I felt like a stranger in a house full of relatives that I wasn't related to. I remember family movie nights that would only happen when I was grounded from watching TV. Instead, I'd be tasked with cleaning the kitchen while the entire family enjoyed the new "Avengers" movie. I remember so vividly crawling around on the floor with a rag and bucket of soapy water as I'd have to 'mop' the entire kitchen floor with a rag. The process took over an hour as I was so afraid of missing a spot and getting yelled at because of it. If I happened to glance in the direction of the TV, they'd yell at me to keep working. That night, I remember looking up at them, rag in hand, wondering if they would even miss me if I snuck out the back door and didn't return.

Life dragged on as the abuse started again. Things gradually returned to how they were before. My dad and stepmom would yell at me for not cleaning properly or missing a spot on the floor while my stepbrother could literally half-ass everything and get all the things he wanted. He would do 'his part' of the kitchen, missing all kinds of shit on the floor and the counter, and would never get the interrogation I would for missing one small speck on a single dish. I didn't know how to make them happy. I was trying so hard, and I was exhausted all the time with nothing to help me cope. I tried to go the extra mile and clean the bathroom too without being told to. Instead of thanking me or even acknowledging that I did it, they would have my stepbrother come in behind me and clean it to make sure it was 'actually clean'. They would find any and every flaw in the work I did and use it as ammunition to say I was intentionally trying to hurt them.

"You didn't use the right cleaner!"
"Why did you miss this smudge on the floor?"
"You're doing this on purpose to hurt the family, aren't you?"

    I didn't know how to please them. Finally, it reached a breaking point. One night, after a long fight between my stepmom, dad, and I, over another spot I missed in the kitchen, my parents forced me to sleep on an extra mattress in my father's room while my stepmom slept in my bed. They planned to keep me home from school so I could 'learn my lesson' and clean the entire house. This was something that had happened before because my stepmom would always make my father choose between her or me as if I was the reason why her new marriage wasn't going to plan. We were fighting and yelling at each other until 5am that morning and two hours later, my stepmom tried to wake me up to get started on all the chores they wanted me to do that day. I physically couldn't get up. I was so mentally, emotionally, and now physically exhausted that I couldn't move. I was so stressed and worn out by the chores and fighting the night before that her attempts to get me up off the mattress didn't work. She got so mad that I wouldn't get up and started yelling at me. I tried to explain that I physically couldn't, and she got even more furious. My dad had already left for the day, taking the other kids to school. I was alone with a monster.

Finally, after I didn't move, she went to the foot end of the mattress, flipped it upward, and pushed it forward, slamming me against the desk behind me. I still have a bump on my head from this incident. I was in shock for about thirty seconds as the mattress fell back to its original position. After it hit the ground, I looked up at my red-faced stepmom and, with all the courage I could muster, called her a bitch. I held her gaze as she came in closer, asking me what I had called her. As I repeated myself, she leaned in closer and started slapping me over and over. She didn't stop until I got up and we both started yelling at each other. After at least thirty minutes of yelling, we decided to go to separate rooms. She went into one room, and I went the opposite direction.

I remember feeling so worthless in that moment. I felt like the universe had betrayed me and that I was alone in a place I was supposed to call home. Tears would fall from my eyes and quickly melt into my pillow every night before I fell asleep. Thoughts of suicide would come, and I would try to shove them away, thinking that it would only make the whole situation worse. I was a worthless burden to my family, and I had no clue how to help them love me.

Then, a letter came in the mail. Apparently, it was an important one because this was the first one that my father and stepmother read to me. I found out later that they kept all the letters and cards my mom would send. Christmas cards, Happy Birthday cards, Thinking of You cards.

Everything, they kept from me so I

wouldn't want to contact my mom. Even on the rare occasion that I would want to call her, they would record the entire phone call, play it back while I was with them, and question me like it was an interrogation. Looking back, I guess they were afraid of me telling her how things really were with them and that it might spur on a call to the Department of Human Services.

The letter was from my mom. She was asking if I wanted to come visit her. I was taken aback by it because I hadn't heard anything from her consistently as my father and stepmother had apparently been screening her calls. Then, a question from my dad came out of nowhere.

"Do you want to go live with your mom?"

I didn't know what to say. I felt like it was the opposite of what they wanted me to do, but my life had become a living hell, so it was definitely a possibility I wanted to thoughtfully consider. They tried to scare me into staying explaining the "horrors" of going to a bigger school. At this point, I had already gone to four different high schools, so I was used to adjusting to new environments quickly.

They gave me a week to decide. I had to choose between my father and my mother. During this week, they said they wouldn't ask or pester me about it, but that I had to go to my father and tell him directly either way. I didn't know what to do, but the idea of starting over in a new environment, away from all the stress and tension that permeated everything was a welcome idea. I don't know why it took me so long to decide. I guess I wanted to see if there was any glimmer of love left in my relationship with my father and stepmother. As the week went on, I tried to find any speck of hope of a relationship with them.

I couldn't find any love from either of them, so I faced my father and told him I wanted to leave.

Six

A couple of days later, we travelled to Harrison, AR to meet my mom and the family she was living with at the time. Harrison was a rough halfway point and when we arrived, my father and mother met at the courthouse to get a power of attorney signed over from my father to my mother. This document basically gave my mother custody of me, unofficially. I haven't seen the document myself, but it was something to the effect that my mom can make decisions for me and act on my behalf.

Then, we moved from the courthouse to the nearby Walmart parking lot and made the 'move'. We moved what little belongings my father and stepmother hadn't taken from me which was basically just my clothes and a few things from my childhood and headed to Springfield, Missouri. I remember hugging my father for the last time that day. I remember feeling how cold and disconnected it felt and realizing, perhaps for the first time, how distant we had become.

Springfield, Missouri was a fresh start, a clean slate. I remember being incredibly nervous as I met the family my mother was living with. My mom had struggled to provide for herself ever since the divorce and had been in and out of homeless shelters and roommate situations for years. It was hard for me to trust that she was going to provide what I needed as I knew she had struggled to take care of her own needs. Nevertheless, this new "adopted family" became a home for me as I worked to complete my high school years.

At this point, I was halfway through my junior year and I remember having such a longing to get out on my own so I could just be myself and live my life with the peace I knew I deserved. The family my mother lived with really became like a family to me and I'm grateful for the things they provided to me. I remember playing catch with the father and getting really into Nova 3, a smartphone first person shooter game, similar to Halo, that we would go to Hy-Vee and play every Sunday evening. Being in that supportive situation really allowed me to believe that I was worthy of the love I so desperately wanted to have in my life.

The support I experienced manifested in my involvement in extra-curricular activities at school. I joined the Men's Chorus right after arriving at Parkview High School. One choir became three my senior year as I leaned into my talents and abilities that had gone dormant. I found my voice and used it, not only in the choir, but in speech and debate. I went on to win awards for my musical, speech, and acting ability throughout my senior year. This was a mountaintop moment for me as I really discovered my worth in an environment that was, finally, one that allowed me to thrive. I'm so thankful for the teachers and mentors that came alongside me during this time and helped me cultivate my talents and truly grow. Rita Johnson, William

Grega, Nancy Wedgeworth, if you're reading this, thank you from the very bottom of my heart.

One of my goals going into my senior year of high school was to, finally, do a sport. I had never done a sport before because of my self-perceived inability to do so. This new freedom to jump into things I enjoyed was so exhilarating that I began to think a sport might be possible. I chose Cross-Country, mostly because it didn't require any level of hand-eye coordination. All you had to do is run. I had always struggled a bit in gym class, but I thought running would be a great way to start being a bit more active. I fell in love with it and even placed in a few races as a junior varsity runner.

My most memorable experience from my high school years was my graduation. In the months leading up to it, the school, rather than requiring the Valedictorian or Salutatorian to make the speech, had tryouts for commencement speaker. While nervous, I was also determined to leave my mark on the school that had, quite literally, changed my life for good. So, I crafted, edited, crafted again, and edited again, a speech that became a speech so memorable and touching that I left the audition room in tears. After the audition, I visited my English professor to ask what he thought. He *secretly* told me that mine was voted as the best one out of the bunch. The sense of pride I felt in that moment was something I had never experienced before.

Graduation day came and I was one of four commencement speakers who delivered funny, heartfelt, and incredible speeches to an arena full of families teachers, administrators and students. I still have the newspaper that was published during that time and look at it occasionally, just to remember how special it was to have such an incredible opportunity.

I was also very involved in the church during this time of my life. It's still difficult for me to talk about my separation from the church because it had once been such a big part of my life, so much so, that I went off to a christian college right after graduation. While my experience with the local church was one of perceived support, it became clear early on in college that my identity as a gay man would not be welcome if I pursued a career as a pastor. I was very deep in the closet and used religion as a cover to dispel any suspicion that I was gay. I cared so deeply for people and hoped to be someone that helped and guided hurting people through some of the most difficult times in their lives. I felt very connected to the mission of Christianity as I thought it was all about helping people.

As I started to wrestle with my identity as a gay man during my second semester, the support I once experienced quickly faded away. I remember having an anxiety attack during a Sunday morning service where I was leading worship. I had jerked off to gay porn the night before and couldn't stop thinking about the double life I was leading. The pressure of perfection in the eyes of people who only wanted to exploit my story for their personal gain was intense and landed me in a mental hospital for suicidal ideation. This was a breaking point that really forced me to consider my identity. I felt as if all the support I had received from the church and my youth pastor and family was based on a version of myself they wanted me to be instead of who I really was. Yes, I was this kind, empathetic, compassionate, person, something I still am today. I was also a closeted gay man that so desperately wanted to become my true self. I remember being so scared to come out, feeling that, if I did, I would lose everything and be out on the street for good.

The week before I went off to college, after forcing my mother to leave earlier that year, the family I was living with also forced me to leave. While I was busy packing everything up to leave, they were also very demanding in what they wanted me to do. A long list a chores appeared as if it was "repayment" for my living there the last several months. After I told them that I wasn't able to mee their demands with everything going on, they told me to leave. The feeling of abandonment I felt in that moment was intense and led me to a very dark place of thinking I did not belong anywhere. If my own, and now, a second family, had abandoned me, what was wrong with me?

    I remember walking to a nearby park, tears streaming down my face the entire time. The first person I called was my youth pastor. I had volunteered a lot at the church and became very close to him. Thirty minutes later, he was there to help me load everything into his vehicle, and move into the spare bedroom at his parent's house. During the next week, I got to know him and his family a bit before going off to college at MidAmerica Nazarene University. The love and care I experienced during that time was so palpable and tangible, something I had never experienced before. They truly became my family and cared for me in so many ways. That first semester at MidAmerica, I would come home for Thanksgiving and Christmas, spending the holidays just like any other normal family. I felt, and in many ways, still feel, indebted to them for how much they did for me. They took me in and treated me like I was their own in such a tangible way. After I published my first book, "Running Home", I was so inspired and touched by the love they provided that I almost began a project entitled "Tangible Grace" that would recount the love and support they so graciously offered me and the profound impact it had on my young life.

  Still, I recount this time in my life with a great deal of hesitation as there was a large part of myself I hid from them, hoping they wouldn't discover my identity as a gay man. I had such a powerful story that would've been so useful as a pastor that I had focused so much of my energy on hiding the other parts of my story I didn't want them to see. I didn't want them to see that I was addicted to gay porn. I didn't want them to see that this was the reason why I left home. They saw a version of myself that I struggled to believe was true and I tried so hard to live up to that.

While I have a lot of regrets about all the things I did during this time to make myself seem worthy of the attention and care I was receiving, I still remember it with a lot of joy and love. My youth pastor's family showed me love in a way I had never experienced before and I'm grateful to have found that in such a critical point in my life.

What I am about to share with you is the very first sermon I ever wrote. While I am no longer a believer in the traditional sense of the word when it comes to Christianity and the things it thrusts on its congregations, I am a believer in the good we can see and produce in the world. When I look back on my time in the church, I see a lot of hurting people that just wanted someone or something to tell them that things would get better, their sicknesses might be healed, and their lives had true and lasting meaning. I still believe in the basic humanity and resiliency of human life to impact the lives of others. I don't, however, believe that organized religion has the answers to any of life's deepest problems.

    I share this sermon to show you what I believed at one point in my life and to really illustrate how far I had gone down the rabbit hole of religion. I place the entire thing in italics as I understand that religion can be something quite traumatic for those of us who have been battered, bruised, and abused by it. For me, gospel or worship music is something I can no longer listen to as it instantly takes me back to a place of hatred of myself and a longing to be something I will never be. If any of these themes ring true for you, I encourage you to move through this chapter quickly or omit it altogether.

For those of you still connected to your faith, I am thankful and excited that you decided to pick up my book. I hope this message of hope reminds you of the good things that religion can do, but serves as a cautionary tale of the detriment it can have, the misleading of a young soul into believing that "everything happens for a reason" and how that belief can lead someone to believe things about himself that are false, unfair, and can cause years of self-hatred that are still being undone.

As you read this sermon, I want you to read it through the lens of a closeted, scared, 18-year-old boy that believed his attraction to other men was a part of himself that God couldn't love. The hatred I had for myself I blame squarely on a religion that told me so and a father that expressed his hatred of it so vividly. In my naivety, I believed I was worthless and unworthy because of it. This belief led me to do outrageous and dangerous things to show how worthy I was of God's love. Turns out, I was chasing something that didn't exist all in the name of righteousness.

"Jeremiah wrote a letter from Jerusalem to the elders, priests, and all the people who had been exiled to Babylon by King Nebuchadnezzar. This was after Kind Jehoiachin, the queen mother, the court officials, the other officials of Judah, and all the craftsmen and artisans had been deported from Jerusalem. He sent the letter with Elasah son of Shaphan and Gemariah son of Hilkiah when they went to Babylon as King Zedikiah's ambassadors to Nebuchadnezzar. This is what Jeremiah's letter said:
'This is what the Lord of Heaven's Armies, the God of Israel, says to all the captives he has exiled to Babylon from Jerusalem: "Build homes and plan to stay. Plant gardens and eat the food they produce. Marry and have children. Then find spouses for them so that

you may have many grandchildren. Multiply! Do not dwindle away. And work for the peace and prosperity of the city where I sent you into exile. Pray to the lord for it, for its welfare will determine your welfare.'

'This is what the Lord of Heaven's Armies, the God of Israel, says: "Do not let your prophets and fortune-tellers who are with you in the land of Babylon trick you. Do not listen to their dreams because they are telling you lies in my name. I have not sent them," says the Lord.

'This is what the Lord says: "You will be in Babylon for seventy years. But then I will come and do for you all the good things I have promised, and will bring you home again. For I know the plans I have for you, says the Lord. They are plans for good and not for disaster, to give you a future and a hope. In those days, when you pray, I will listen. If you look for me wholeheartedly, you will find me. I will be found by you, says the lord. I will end your captivity and restore your fortunes. I will gather you out of the nations where I sent you and will bring you home again to your own land."

This is where I led the congregation in prayer before the message.

Have you ever made plans with someone and it didn't go as well as you wanted it to? I have. There was this one time that I made plans with a girl that I secretly had a 'crush' on.
Sidebar: this was a feeble attempt to silence any rumors that I might, in fact, be gay.
I asked her out for coffee and she said yes. I was thrilled. I spent the days in between

dreaming about what our relationship could become, after this fateful first date.

Okay, I'm cringing so hard right now just reading this… yikes

Then, the day came and I got extremely nervous so I did everything that a guy "should do" for a first date. I reserved us a table at the local Starbucks (turns out they don't do reservations), I bought flowers for her, and even put on my best outfit and cologne. As I pulled into the driveway that afternoon, my heart started pounding in my chest. Luckily, she wasn't there yet so I had a few minutes to gather my thoughts. I walked towards the door and sat down. Then, she walked in sporting a T-Shirt and jeans while I was all dressed up. My face turned red as I looked over at the bouquet of flowers graciously sitting on the table. It was obvious that she did not think this was a date. I was beginning to realize that this wasn't going to turn out the way I had hoped.

Have you ever been there? You know, when something goes horribly wrong and you don't know what to do? You didn't plan for her to think this wasn't a date. I mean, it was supposed to go according to my plan, right? We'd go on a couple of dates, we'd get really close, and then the time would come where I would pop the question.

Super cringe

That's exactly how I wanted it to happen. When things happen in life that we don't completely understand, when things don't go our way, it's hard to see through the chaos what God's plans are. We don't plan for our family to fall apart, we don't plan for our hearts to be broken, and we don't plan for our addiction to get out of control."

Okay, I planned to leave the entire sermon in here, but I literally want to throw up reading all the ridiculous things I believed about life and the mantra of "everything happens according to God's plan" when I had literally been through my own version of hell. *grabs barf bucket*

Needless to say, I was in deep. The girl referenced in the sermon was one of my co-workers at Mardel, a Christian Bookstore I worked at to keep up my 'super Christian' appearance. I was so deep in religion that every single part of my life was a part of it. At school, I would go to Fellowship of Christian Athletes, and I even worked at the largest Christian bookstore in the area. At church, I was the wide-eyed, devoted 'believer' that volunteered every chance I got, was on the worship team, designed and ran the visuals during worship, and did literally anything the church asked me to. When they suggested I go to a Christian college, it felt like the logical next step.

    At this point in the retelling of my first book, I'm skipping two chapters that detail severe delusions about what I considered to be witnessing opportunities that were actually experiences that could've put me in very real danger. I detail an experience with a homeless man I met at Waffle House that I later gave a ride home to and took to church the following Sunday. While I didn't consider him dangerous, the thought that this was a 'God thing' and I should willingly put myself in danger at the very vulnerable age of 18 is something

I won't soon forget. It was things like this that I remember in retrospect that could've had very real implications on my safety, all in the name of evangelism.

This is what religion did to me. I never felt like I was doing enough to be worthy of love from a supposed God that loved me only if I did enough. Only if I prayed enough. Only if I went to every church service. Only if I went to church camp. Only if I went to a Christian college. Only if I wasn't gay.

Religion had a planned attack on my heart to find the thing I hated about myself, make me constantly think about it, and use it against me for free labor, exploit my story for money, and really use every part of my being against me to plunge me deeper into a belief that God will 'save' me from the very thing religion made me hate about myself.

seven

Now for something a bit lighter. While my first book contained a lot of religious jargon intertwined with my personal "testimony" I also had a few passages where I recounted big moments in my young life. One of those moments was when I got my first car.

Weeks before I bought it, I had been shopping around on Craigslist to no avail. All the cars were either really cheap and sketchy, or they were out of my price range entirely. I was beginning to get discouraged. Then it dawned on me. I could apply for a loan! It might be a long shot, but the worst they could say is no, right?

The search began the day after the light bulb came on. I started with the bank that currently supplied my checking account. I had high hopes, as I had been with the bank for about three years. I though I had established a working relationship with them, but I was still quite young and nieve. When I went in to apply for a loan, the branch manager was so kind and courteous. She really knew how to give great customer service, and by the time I left, I really believed that I might have a chance.

The next day, I was supposed to get a phone call from the manager telling me whether or not I got approved. I didn't get the call, so I went in and talked to her in person. I hung my head as she, politely as she could, told me that I was not approved. I was crushed. As I was pulling out of the parking lot, however, I remembered something that my dad had done growing up. When he got a loan for our house, he had shopped around for a bank. He wanted to get the ebst deal, and the best interest rate. So, I set out on a journey to find a bank that would give me a loan for my first car.

    Finally, I landed at a local bank that had only a few locations in the Springfield area. After getting denied at so many other banks, the loan officer referred me to this one. She gave me the name and phone number of one of the loan officers that she knew personally. It sounded great and I was so excited! I called the guy the same day and ended up setting an appointment with him scheduled for the following Monday. The time in-between was full of excitement and anxiety as I really needed a car. It was early fall and the cold winter months were approaching. My 49cc scooter was not winter proof, and was definitely on its last leg.

Monday morning, I walked through the doors of the bank, dressed up and ready to give my "I desperately need a car" speech. I checked in with the receptionist, and sat down after getting a free cup of coffee from the little kiosk by the door. I had practiced what I would say on the way over and was starting to get a little nervous.

"I have a scooter that is not winter proof."

"I think it might be on its last leg."

"Please help me...*falls to knees*"

These were just a few phrases that I wanted to incorporate in my loan pitch. Finally, as I finished my cup of coffee, the receptionist came out from the back and told me that, the loan officer I was supposed to meet with had tried to get ahold of me in order to reschedule because something came up. I didn't receive a phone call or email from him, cancelling our meeting.

I went on to ask the receptionist if there was someone else that I might be able to meet with. Monday was my only day off that week, and I wanted to get the ball rolling before the winter months set in. The receptionist said that there were other loan officers available that would be able to help me so I waited just a few minutes until one was available.

The loan officer that I ended up

speaking with was the most chipper loan officer I have ever met. It was a welcome surprise after all of the banks I had been to at this point. She was so happy that I had thought to come to their bank to get a loan for my first car. I filled out the application and I was approved for the loan the same day. As we were finishing up the paper work, she asked if I had found a car yet. At this point, I hadn't actually found a specific car, but I knew the price range that I could afford with my small paychecks from Mardel. I told her that I hadn't and she perked up a little. She went on to tell me that she was looking to sell her personal car that she had had for seven plus years. I asked her what kind of car it was and as soon as she said, "It's a 2003 Honda Accord, 2-door coup, V6", my ears perked up. It almost sounded too good to be true. I asked her how much she wanted for it and she said that she would call her husband at lunch to talk to him about it. Then, we agreed that she would call me after and let me know.

At this point, I was already starting to downplay the whole thing. I thought she would want too much for it, or something would go wrong with the loan. I was expecting my first car to be a total clunker. This car was not a clunker. Before I left, she took me on a test drive of it. She offered to let me drive, but I declined because it had been so long since I had driven an actual car. I was afraid I might wreck it before I even got it out of the parking lot. Thankfully, she understood and drove herself. As I opened the car door, my eyes got really big. It was so nice and I didn't think for a minute I could afford this. It had leather, heated seats, a CD changer, a sunroof, and was any young boys dream. It was just sporty enough while being practical that I thought it would fit my personality perfectly.

After the test drive, we came back to the bank and went inside. She had heard back from her husband and told me that she would sell the car for exactly what the bank would loan me for it. I was totally blown away. I was incredibly excited and called my youth paster's dad and told him everything that happened. He was very excited for me and told me he would give me a ride to the closing the following Wednesday.

eight

After dropping out of college, I tried so hard to be successful in anything and everything. I had big dreams to be successful and I took very extreme measures that landed me in a difficult place. After starting my first full-time position at a local bank, I took a big step to move out of my adopted family's home, a place that had become a wonderful comfort and healing for me after leaving college.

Looking back to the months after leaving, I cannot thank them enough for keeping me together and focused. I was so lost and depressed for several months, so much so that I had to sit down each night and write an incredibly detailed list of what I needed to do to function the next day. Items on the list included: get up, make bed, eat breakfast, shower, etc. They did not give up on me. What a wonderful expression of love they showed to me.

That season was the start of a crisis of faith that would last for several years. I know I was not in a good place, but they accepted and loved me right where I was and did not for a moment think that I was a lost cause. They were so wonderful to me and treated me like I belonged even as I believed I did not. I cannot thank them enough for everything they did for me, showing me love in a way I had never experienced before.

During this time of my life, there was an immense longing to be independent that drove a lot of my decisions. I had a sense of guilt for everything that my adopted family had so freely given to me that I knew I would never be able to repay. Countless nice dinners out, wonderful gifts, cups of coffee, trips to Silver Dollar City, and free rent and utilities that I could not pay for myself, not to mention all the wonderful dinners Mrs. Fay would cook for everyone. I wanted so badly to show them that I could do this thing called life and that I would not have to rely on them. Since then, I have learned that love does not count the cups of coffee drank or the number of chips that you eat from the bag. Sharing life together contains within it an inherent quality of forgetting the physical cost of things, knowing that connecting with each other is what truly matters. I understand this concept now, but I did not back then. I hope to show this great compassion and love in the same way to someone in the future to somehow repay the wonderful love and provision they so generously offered me.

As someone who grew up almost entirely in the church (and by entirely, I mean leading worship and even preaching a bit in my later years), I can tell you that there are good things about the church, but there are also some very bad things that I witnessed that completely turned me away from it. I remember the moment I came face to face with the rejection of my identity as a gay man.

I had gone off to college and

was attending a Christian university, majoring in ministry. It was my second semester, and the pressure of ministry was hitting me quite hard. I was leading worship for a church close by as a part of a small ministry team. Every Sunday, we would go to this small community church and our team would basically run the church. Week after week, my anxiety would grow that someone might find out that I was gay. A quick look at my phone browser history would've confirmed any suspicions. My love for other people was visible on my face and in how I interacted with people, but my identity that was starting to seep out terrified me. I remember my first anxiety attack happened during a worship set on a Sunday morning at that church. I was mid-song, and I couldn't catch my breath. I couldn't breathe and the vocalist that sang with me had to take over the song. My heart was pounding so hard in my chest, and I couldn't even get the words out to say that we were taking up the offering next. Chords stopped making sense on the guitar I held in my hands, and I had a complete meltdown in my mind as I stood there. I muscled through and somehow was able to get through the next song before sitting down for the sermon. What I didn't know was that moment was just the beginning.

After that experience, I voluntarily stepped down from the worship team and had a massive time of introspection. This thing that I was chasing, this hope to "change people's lives" was right there staring me in the face. This thing that told me I couldn't be gay and change people's lives at the same time. This thing that I had prayed and prayed and prayed and prayed for God to take from me, never left and the voices that told me I was a fraud swirled in my mind.

The homophobia that I experienced externally slowly started to seep into every part of my being, to a point where I completely hated myself. I tried so hard to cover up who I was with religion, that I had created this façade of holiness that I took into my teen, and later, adult years. I thought that if I could pray enough or have enough faith that somehow God would "fix" me and make me into the person that I hoped to become. I attended church every time the doors were open and became incredibly involved in every aspect of it. I had painted a picture that I wanted everyone to see, but on the inside, this hatred of myself was ripping me apart.

Then, I would hear messages of condemnation that would only deepen the loathing I had for myself. At a few different points during this period of my life, I opened up to some of my pastors about it, hoping that they could somehow help me through the pain I was experiencing. The reality was, though, that most did not have anything to offer other than gentle condemnation. My desperate search for someone who could understand what I was experiencing inside met dead end after dead end and left me more helpless than before. Still, I tried to muster an outward appearance of redemption into a person separate from my sexuality, hoping that eventually that image would morph itself into my actual reality. I was so desperate to create my identity separate from who I really was that I published my first book in hopes that people would genuinely believe that I had overcame homosexuality. The reality was, however, that this aching to belong and become who I really am was tearing me apart on the inside.

    The next few weeks, I floated through my classes, trying to find a way to make both work in my mind, but all I could hear were the voices of condemnation and shame showered on by my professors, pastors, and supposed mentors that were supposed to be the "loving" people I should look up to. These were the same people that bragged in the dorm hallways and showers about who they banged the night before, who's breast they held and how big they were, and all the things that were supposedly "okay" if you were a heterosexual male and had enough money to cover it up. All these thoughts culminated in an even bigger anxiety attack that occurred when I was alone in my dorm room. This one was bigger than the last. I couldn't breathe, I started hyperventilating and lost control of my hands. They started to seize up and contort into deformed claws that I just couldn't stop staring at. Even as I was having this anxiety attack, the voices of condemnation in my head told me that I shouldn't feel this way, how dare I let myself get this low, how dare I let everyone down that had worked so hard to get me to this prestigious school. How dare I give up the ministry scholarship I had been so graciously offered. How dare I give up the opportunity to study at such an expensive, prestigious, school that had reluctantly allowed a teenage runaway to grace their campus and halls.

This spiral led to my first suicide attempt, just a few weeks after the first anxiety attack. I had full bottle of Excedrin in my dorm room that was just staring me in the face. I kept looking at it, thinking all it would take was a tall glass of water. If that didn't work, wrapping the phone cord next to my bed around my neck would. I was in full spiral as I wrestled with a dream that was falling apart in front of me.

The college itself found the need to justify my attendance by exploiting me for my story to raise money for the university. During my first semester, I was approached by the university advancement office to share my story with the president of the university. At the time, I was honored that they would even think of me. I was young and naïve, not thinking about what they were really doing. I remember being in a room with several professional cameras on me and a big, black sheet background behind me. I was vulnerable and shared my entire story of how I left home and how the church supposedly saved me from the "wrong path" carefully leaving out the fact that I was gay. I said all the right things, how much the university meant to me and how excited I was to be there. What I didn't know at the time, is that they were going to use that video to send to churches to guilt people into giving money to the university. I guess it was just the right kind of story they could use to exploit money from people for their personal gain. Meanwhile, I was left with almost twenty thousand dollars of student loan debt when I left during my second semester. I felt violated and taken advantage of. I felt like I was almost emotionally and spiritually raped. They took my story, sold it, and plunged me into thousands of dollars of debt I may never be able to pay back.

 Somehow, even after that terrible experience, I still believed in a God who loved me. Looking back, I was so stupid to, but I'll digress for now. Even after leaving college, I still attended church and stayed involved in it for a long time. When I dropped out of school, I moved back to what was then home and went back to the church that had so excitedly sent me off to college. I felt as if I had let everyone down and felt completely ashamed that I was back. The leadership of the church had changed hands, and I became more involved in the church than ever. I was on almost all the teams and wanted so desperately to show that I wasn't a lost cause.

I knew I needed to work through everything that I had experienced so I went to the new lead pastor to seek wise counsel. He was someone who was on mood stabilizers and a few other medications for mental health, so I felt safe talking to him about what I was experiencing. The first few counseling sessions were fine and allowed me to open up a bit. I shared some very difficult things that I had experienced; family things, social things, my disappointment about dropping out, etc.

Then, as the weeks passed, we progressed into deeper topics and eventually landed on my sexuality. By this point, I had established a sense of trust with him, thinking that he would listen and offer help. That's what it was at first, until we arrived at this topic. I told him that I had experienced these "urges" that I couldn't get out of my head. He wanted me to go into full detail about the urges I was experiencing, and he even asked me about when I think about guys, what exactly I would do to them sexually. I told him and what I was met with was comments of shame, the revoking of my local minister's license and subtle reminders of what the church denomination believed about same sex relationships. All of those were to be expected, but cut very deeply, just another reminder that I couldn't do what I thought was my "calling".

    The Sunday following that conversation was something out of my worst nightmares. Normally, when I would walk into church, I would be greeted by all my friends with hugs and a happy "Nice to see you!" This Sunday was different. Almost everyone looked at me with hesitation and found a reason to move away from me. Church elders that would smile and greet me no longer wanted anything to do with me. I had been outed to the entire church, or just the people that led things, I couldn't tell. Everyone seemed to know, and I was absolutely mortified. In the weeks that followed, I was pulled off the worship team, no longer ran the slides in the back, and slowly disconnected from everything about the church. I was so mortified and upset that I left to another church, stupidly, in the same denomination.

I tried to get involved in the same way at this one, but it just felt so different now. My story had been ripped from me, exploited for money, and now outed to the congregation that was supposed to love and support me. I felt alone in a room full of people I thought I knew, and I felt completely betrayed.

Since this mortifying experience, I have left the church entirely. In my previous book, I touched on the few experiences I've had since then, moments of still trying to make religion work in my life and the miserable failures that resulted from those attempts. Now, I distance myself from religious people, knowing full well what they do to people and the harm they have the potential to cause. I don't buy it anymore and I hope that my story saves someone from the horrifying experience I endured. Religious people prey on your hopes and dreams, promising you a better life if you give everything to a higher power. What they don't tell you is that you're really giving everything to the religious leaders; pastors, worship leaders, etc. and get judgement and rejection in return. They shake you down for your money and your story, use it for their gain, and discard you like week old spaghetti. It's not right, and I will live the rest of my life trying to expose this truth in hopes of saving people from the disorienting experience I endured. Needless to say, I don't buy it.

nine

After dropping out, I needed to find something to do. A few weeks passed painfully slow as I tried to make sense of my situation. All the excitement surrounding my graduation, acceptance into college, and the big move to 'leave the nest' had faded and I was incredibly depressed. I remember having to make checklists of things I needed to do, just to ensure I would get them done. The checklist would include get up, make bed, brush teeth, take a shower, and other simple tasks that seemed like mini Everests. I remember it being so hard to believe in myself after all the momentum I had in my senior year. I had never hit the ground so hard in my life.

One of my first glimmers of hope was my first full time job at a bank as a Customer Service Representative. It was a difficult job, helping people with their bank accounts, something people tend to get REALLY emotional about.

The job at the bank did not work out and I found myself in a sticky situation. I was struck with such freedom that I was overwhelmed by the offers of credit and financial traps for which I mistook for freedom. In 2016,

I went from one job to another trying to find something that I would want to do for the rest of my life.

Now, in interviews, I find myself calling this my "Year of Discovery" to explain away my short track records at various positions. I stumbled across hospitality during this time after walking into a nearby hotel. It was a failing hotel that did not seem to have a clear and focused management team. I helped in any way I could but did not last long after becoming frustrated with the lack of competent management. Now, I look at this season with a little more emotional intelligence, seeing that I could have handled a few things a lot better that year.

One day, I decided to update my resume and walk into an upscale hotel down the road from the house I was renting. I printed my experience on fancy paper, hoping to portray the confidence that I was trying to muster. After a wonderful interview, sharing my disappointment of dropping out of college and starting over, I was hired as a front desk agent. It was here that I discovered a passion for serving people and providing hospitality to a myriad of guests and visitors. It was during this same time that I became personally and financially stressed. This among other things moved me to leave the church I was attending and attend a church that was planted at the hotel where I worked. It was closer and helped me save gas. It did seem, at times, that I did not leave the hotel because my days off were Sunday and Wednesday and on these days, I would come right back to my place of employment.

During this time, I also felt myself falling into yet another depression. I had a friend from high school move into the second bedroom of the house that I was trying to "buy". I was trying to do too much too fast, and I buried myself. The roommate situation did not work very well, especially after I invited my mother to live with me as well. I did a lot of stupid and desperate things that year to try to get ahead and keep the commitments that I had made. When it all fell apart, I was exhausted and did not know what to do. My roommate moved out and stopped paying rent and I could not handle caring for my mother while I was working to support myself. It was all too much and the pressure of it all mounted quickly. I ended up losing my job at the hotel in September and spent several days completely depressed and hiding out at home. I found it hard to even leave my bed. A similar episode to what had happened while I was still in college. I knew what it was, but I did not know how to stop myself from going to that dark place of emotional numbness that dulled my reality.

I remember hearing knocks on the door as I hid away in my bedroom, not wanting to face the embarrassing situation I had found myself in. Several people from the church tried so hard to help me, but I was unable to find it within myself to fully connect with God in a way that had some resemblance of holiness. I felt completely empty and dull. I was not sure how to shake it off. My situation was hopeless, and I felt completely out of sorts. I am thankful for the people around me that tried to help lift me out of the dullness I was facing. At that point, I do not think there was anything they could have said or did that would've had any effect on my mental fog and confusion. I needed a fresh start, a chance to try again. That chance came during a meeting with my adopted dad at Culver's on a sunny afternoon. I did not know how to talk to him after I had ignored his advice and moved out on my own and completely messed everything up. His advice was simple, yet effective. I needed to move back closer to family. I needed to reach out and re-connect.

A new start began with a U-Haul and boxes that smelled of grocery items from the Walmart down the street. My adopted father graciously offered to rent the U-Haul and move me to Jonesboro, Arkansas where my sister had offered to let me stay in one of the rent houses her and my brother-in-law owned. Several trips to the U-Haul and boxes later, it was packed, and we started the approximately five-hour journey from Springfield, Missouri to Jonesboro, Arkansas.

I remembered this place from growing up, but so much had changed that it seemed like a totally different place. I remember arriving at the house and my mind swimming as I looked around at the condition of the house that my sister had allowed me to stay in. It wasn't nice, there were holes in the floor, the fridge only partially worked, and the space heaters barely kept me warm as the winter months began. That night I went out to the local neighborhood market to get something to drink and find some sense of normalcy. When I got back from the short trip, I fought back tears as I looked around at all the boxes and the state in which my life had ended up.

I had a laptop that had all my music on it and I began to listen to various artists. Music has always held a special place in my heart and at this moment it seemed to help lift me out of myself. I started unpacking, cleaning, and getting my life back together. It was so hard to think that I was not a complete failure. I had messed everything up and had to start again. With my prior, yet short, hospitality experience, I updated my resume and printed it at the local Fed-Ex Office store. Within 2 weeks, I found a night audit position at a local hotel. It was income and was a position that allowed me to reflect on what had happened. I started to heal through the long nights of financial reports and sliding folios under guestroom doors. It was not hard work, but it was something to keep me going.

Eventually, I was promoted to the second shift, 3-11, after several guests had commented on the level of customer service I provided on online reviews. I was excited to welcome guests to our hotel and take good care of them. I discovered a heart that longed to make people welcome and happy, especially those who would stay during a funeral or difficult family situation. I remember several personal letters I wrote to guests who mentioned at check-in that they had just lost a loved one or had a family member in the hospital. It was these moments that I longed to provide comfort to these guests, helping them to see that everything would be okay. I started getting personal notes left for me at the desk almost weekly from guests who appreciated all my assistances. These notes meant the world to me. I still have most of them.

During this time, I was very particular about my financial situation. I was able to pay off my car rather quickly, keeping tabs on everything and making sure I knew where my money was going. What a relief it was to mail the last money order to the bank. I was so excited that day. Life moved on steadily as I worked at the hotel. Once I was employed, I started paying rent and took over utilities for the property. I was making it, barely, but I was making it.

A couple of months went by as I continued working at the hotel. During this time, I had reconnected with my grandmother and several members of my family that I had lost contact with. We would meet up every Saturday at the nursing home and have lunch with my grandma. It was a little awkward at first, but Saturday after Saturday it got easier and easier to share life together. I regained my relationship with my family on my mother's side, something that was missing in my life. It seemed to fill the void of parents that was gaping and eating my emotional state alive. Eventually, I was making enough to be able to move out of the house that I was renting from my sister and brother-in-law.

I moved into a one-bedroom apartment just across town. It was a nice living community with fountains and amenities that I could utilize. I was so excited to have working appliances and central heat and air, something that I had missed from the house in Springfield. The family members I had grown close to helped me move from the house into the apartment. I enjoyed decorating the apartment and seemed to settle in nicely. A few months later, I resigned from my position at the hotel after management changed and seemed to drop the ball on a lot of things. I am glad that I left when I did because shortly after I did, the managers were escorted off the property for committing fraudulent activity. During that time, I had done a lot to ensure that everything was taken care of. I strived to take care of guests in the best way that I could and had numbers to prove it. After the management team changed, a position was created for Front Desk Supervisor. I applied with extensive information as to why I would be a great fit for the position. I printed off guest reviews that raved about the level of service I provided and about how many people I had enrolled into the hotel rewards program. I thought for sure I would get it, but I did not and am thankful now that I didn't. I updated my resume and sent it out to several hotels around Jonesboro. I finally landed a breakfast/front desk position at another nearby hotel. I absolutely loved taking care of everyone and making sure they had what they needed. I enjoyed delighting little kids with a special sucker or coloring page only if they finished their food at breakfast. I really enjoyed it, but it was only part time and I was not able to pay my bills with what I had coming in. I really wanted to stay with the hotel, but they understood my reasoning when I left.

A phone call for an interview came for an office coordinator position at a nearby staffing agency. I met with a wonderful staffing consultant, not knowing it was for an internal position, but desperately needed help finding something.

After sharing my employment journey, a second interview by phone was set up with the owner. I was nervous because this was a big deal, and I was not sure if I would be good at the job. I was cautiously confident in my abilities but was not sure how they would transfer to the staffing environment. I got the job and started in on very extensive training and development. The job consisted of being the hub of communication for the office ensuring that everyone communicated successfully. It was a really good job and I enjoyed having the opportunity to see applicants through the application, interview, and hiring process. I was able to see firsthand lives change from the front window. I grew close with several of my coworkers and really enjoyed getting to know them. A few weeks after I started, there was an annual floating trip to a property my boss owned on a nearby river.

It was a time of refreshment for each of us after the strain of our daily chaos. For the first time in a long time, I had fun.

Slowly but surely, I started noticing my inadequacies for the position I was holding. The sheer amount of phone calls coming in became too much for me to handle and I would get stressed out easily. It did not help that I was facing mental illness and the internal fight with my sexuality that I did not know how to face or have the tools to even start the process of navigating this part of my life. Mental illness is very prevalent in my family and I knew that I would have to struggle with this. I finally found a medication that would assist me and provide relief from the possible bipolar disorder I was facing. I would have seasons of elation that would lead me to believe that I could do anything and everything and do it perfectly to days that I had to drag myself out of bed because I could not bear to face another day.

The stress and demands of the position became too much for me to handle and I broke in the form of a phone call one day. I was so ashamed and upset with myself that I had allowed myself to treat someone the way I did. I did not represent the company in the professional manner I had strived to.

A new start began with an apron and breakfast food. I returned to the hotel and started working part time as a breakfast attendant and part time on the front desk. Within a month, I had been mentioned several times by guests and was moved from breakfast to full time front desk. A few more weeks went by and a position was created for a Front

Office Supervisor. I remember the day very fondly. I was cleaning up in the kitchen after our evening manager's reception and the manager came in and asked me what I thought about becoming the Front Office Supervisor. It came with a raise and the opportunity to not only make a difference in the lives of our guests, but in the lives of my coworkers as well. I was so excited and absolutely loved it.

We had an extraordinarily strong team and we strived to take care of our guests in a way that would inspire them to come back. I watched as the team I managed grew and grew and became more confident in their ability to take care of our guests in a way that mattered. I helped them see that hospitality matters and that the guests that we served were real people that just needed to know that we cared. In the weeks before I released my position there, several things happened that hurt and alienated me from the hospitality industry. My boss and his assistant were both terminated, and our director of sales had accepted another position at a new property being built in the area. That season of my life was extremely difficult because I tried to keep my front desk team focused on what we were there to do and help them see that we would make it even when we did not know what the future for our hotel would hold.

The responsibilities of my position became more and more of a burden on my life than ever before. The property management company sent several interim employees to help us during this time, but most had to be caught up to speed very quickly on what was going on at our property so they would know how to manage everything for the week that they were there. A new week would come, and another interim GM would be there. During this time, positions opened for Director of Sales, Assistant GM, and GM. I applied to both Director of Sales and Assistant GM to show that I was open to however the company might want to use my skills and abilities.

The positions began to be filled and I was not considered for any of them. I was offered a small raise after everything I had done to try to keep the hotel together in the absence of consistent management. It hurt because I worked so hard to show that I was able to do it. I did not care what position it was, I just wanted to help and to see our hotel succeed. This situation led me to leave my position there rather abruptly, mostly because it hurt so much. I cared about each person that I served and worked with, but I had to find some way to move on and move forward and I could not face the heartbreak of telling each one goodbye.

The pressure in my last few weeks at the hotel brought me to examine myself and really search for the true me and it was in this time that I publicly came out as gay on Facebook. Most were incredibly supportive of my decision to open up about this part of my life and some were not. I desperately wanted to be happy because I was not. I had a wonderful job, a nice apartment, a loving dog, and everything that you would think would make someone happy and I was still miserable inside. I did not know how to deal with these feelings of attraction to the same sex that I had and tried to hide since I was 10. Coming out was the beginning of a long journey in accepting myself and discovering what happiness would look like for me.

The job search began, and I was disillusioned and very discouraged, wondering what to do next. I applied several places and got no responses from any of them. I even tried to start my own business with my publishing and design skills that I gained from classes in high school. I prospected for several weeks talking to business owners about their publishing and design needs and even designed a few logos. All of this did not go anywhere, and I found myself evicted, losing several things that I had held dear.

Turbulence followed in the coming months as I searched for something that I could see myself pursuing for the rest of my life. At this point, I had tried so many different things, I felt like I would never find what I was meant to do. My resume still contains multiple pages of positions I have held for short periods of time. I have gained a lot of experience, and I now kind of chuckle at it thinking of how Albert Einstein discovered so many ways how not to make a light bulb before finding the one that worked.

I still had not been able to fully reconcile my faith and my sexuality, stumbling over a church that was openly affirming of the LGBTQIA+ community. When I started attending, I was not fully sure of who I was yet, but I knew that I needed a space to figure it out. During this time, I was very financially stressed, mostly because I had chosen a place to live that I could not afford, and it wrecked my financial situation. Still, I tried to hold true to my faith, eventually leading the church in worship as I had done several times before. I loved it and found a sense of purpose and belonging there, but some of my family members were less than understanding and all but disowned me for attending. Family members I had grown close to said nothing as others barred me from visiting their house. Once again, I was an alien and did not belong. I tried attending another church and getting involved, but when one of the ministers made a pass at me, I decided that I could no longer entertain the thought of a God who would allow me to carry so much pain. This battle between my sexuality and my faith was unrelenting and led me to leave the church entirely.

It was not worth the mental torment that went on inside my head as I so desperately tried to prove that I was a good person to people who were convinced otherwise.

I continued to struggle within myself to find who I truly was. The war inside my mind between my sexuality and spirituality continued to take its toll on every part of my life. I was exhausted all the time, trying to figure out how to reconcile everything. Then something happened that changed my perspective entirely. It was mid-August, and I got a text message from a close family member that said that my grandmother was in the hospital. Leading up to this, because of the global pandemic, visitations with her had been reduced to seeing her through the window at the nursing home. Before this, Saturdays were so full of joy as my uncle, cousin, great aunt, and sister would meet at the nursing home every Saturday and have lunch. Grandma would always save half a sandwich and/or a cookie for me and have it waiting for me when I got there. I would almost always be late because I was exhausted from work. She was understanding and was always ready to give me a big hug when I got there. I had gotten so used to our Saturdays that the nursing home almost felt like home. I looked forward to seeing my family every week and I could not have prepared myself for what happened next. Seeing her through the window became seeing her in the ICU. Seeing her in the ICU became meeting a nurse at the hospice center asking me if I knew yet or not. My world went dark as I wrote out what I would say at her funeral:

"When I moved to Jonesboro back in 2016, I was lost and felt completely alone. I remember the first time I went out to the nursing center to see her and how happy she was to see me after several years of being apart. That visit was the beginning of several Saturdays spent visiting with her, my uncle, and cousin. I would bring my southwest salad and sweet tea and we would share life together. She was there through promotions, job losses, birthdays, and holidays. She was there when I was trying to figure out what to do with my life and was proud of me regardless. She would always ask how I was doing and wanted to make sure that I was taking care of myself.

Today, I am not really sure what to say. I know I will forever cherish the memories we made early on in my life, but perhaps cherish even more the memories we have made over the past four years. I am so thankful for the circumstances that brought me to Jonesboro in 2016 and will never forget the wonderful times we had together. My grandma was a sweet, loving, and caring soul who never wanted to burden anyone for anything. Maybe that's where I get it from. She had a peace about her that made all the craziness in my life go away. Her hugs would make everything okay. She always wanted to make sure I had enough to eat, even when she was the one who needed to eat the most. She would give me cookies off her nursing home tray, and sometimes save half of her sandwich for me to eat when I got there. She was the best grandma any grandson could ask for and I was lucky to call her mine. We know that she is in a better place and is no longer in pain.

Over the past few weeks, I have not been able to stop asking myself, "Where do I go from here?" How do you move on from losing someone you loved so dearly? I guess that is a question I may never get the answer to. For now, I will keep chasing what makes me happy because I know that that is all she ever wanted for me is to be happy. I will pursue what I'm passionate about and work every day to make my grandmother proud. We love you grandma and life simply won't be the same without you."

Those were the words I mustered together to say at her funeral. I could barely get it out, fighting back tears the whole time. My relationship with God died with her as I watched a beautiful life be reduced to seven boxes of her belongings. My grandmother's death jolted me and made me realize how important it is to find yourself and your happiness in life, regardless of what people might think of you.

Shortly before she passed, I started a journal to help me process this season of my life. On the day that she passed, I wrote the following:

8/25/2020

1:05pm

Dear Grandma,

We lost you today. I was at home about to get ready for work and got the call. You were at the hospice center for a very short amount of time before you passed. We were all there afterwards. When I arrived, the nurse at the desk was so kind and helpful and escorted me to the room. On the way, she introduced me to the chaplain, and he was very kind and gracious as well. When I saw you, I couldn't hold it together. I broke down just a few seconds after walking in the door. You seemed so peaceful and were finally at rest. We sat there for about an hour sharing our favorite memories of you. I talked about all the Saturdays we spent together at the nursing home and how you'd save half a sandwich for me and/or give me the cookie off your tray. I remember those plastic juice boxes you had put orange juice in when I came to see you growing up. I will find one and keep it to remember you by. When I left the hospital on Tuesday, I went to the gift shop and broke down right there in the store. I found this art piece that had "Best Grandma Ever" inscribed on it and bought it for you. I wanted to give it to you, but I wasn't sure if you would know what was going on, so I just kept it.

Thank you for always being so proud of me even when I felt like I had no idea what I was doing with my life. You were there through every job loss, promotion, birthday, and holiday over the past four years and so many more occasions when I was little. I remember taking selfies with you at Thanksgiving just two years ago. That seems like just yesterday. I remember one Saturday at the nursing home when we were visiting, and you said that you were so sorry for the mother I ended up with and how you felt so bad for how things were for me. I cannot tell you how much that meant to me that you recognized the struggles I've been through with less than wonderful parents. I do want you to know that it's not your fault and I turned out okay despite all that happened. I know you know that.

Love,

John

The wind had been knocked out of me. My world was spinning and for weeks I did not know how to move forward. I felt like I was holding on by a thread and losing my grandmother was the jolt that broke the string.

Shortly before my grandmother passed, I had started putting myself out there on dating apps, trying to find the right guy. My first real relationship with a guy was wonderful but came at the wrong time in my life when so many other things clouded my vision and held me back from the life I wanted. I was still in the process of accepting who I was and was trying so hard to do so, but the pain of losing my grandmother made me shove everything away and close off my heart to anyone that wanted in. I took time off work, changed jobs, and truly had to find myself after everything that happened.

    For years, I had been so close to and involved in the church. I would sing in the choir, play piano and guitar, and sing songs about a God that I believed hated me because of my sexuality. It was a toxic relationship and after losing my grandmother, I knew that I had to end it. I didn't realize until I started pulling away from God, how much my life had been wrapped up in this scheme that wanted me to pay someone to tell me to hate myself. I remember going through my books and getting rid of seventy five percent of them because they had Christian themes.

I did not want to hate myself any longer and walking away from the church is what I needed to start loving myself again. Every Christian theme reminded me of a God that did not love me. It reminded me of every message that demonized me and made me out to be a person that I was not. It reminded me of the counseling sessions I experienced that were used to expose my identity to the church. It reminded me of the smashed iPod hanging over the kitchen sink. There are so many damaging messages being perpetuated by the church that if they would just listen to one gay person, sit down with them and listen to their story, maybe they would hear the pain they experience from their hurtful words. If there really is a God, why do we not see it in the eyes of Christians who spread hate about certain people groups they do not like? If this criticism and hatred is what God's love looks like, I don't want it.

Leaving the church was probably one of the most difficult things I have ever done. Church turned me into a crazy person. I would ping-pong back and forth between being super spiritual, and "struggling" with my sexuality. It was exhausting and I always felt like I had to prove how much of a good person I was. I love people and wanted so badly to show that love to people, but so many times it was met with questioning who I was or trying to manipulate me into being who they wanted me to be. I got to a point where I just couldn't do it anymore.

ten

After walking away from the church, I started cleaning house in other areas of my life as well. I have always enjoyed reading and stumbled across a few books that helped me do just that. Marie Kondo's books about tidying your home and life were very influential as I started rooting out anything that did not spark joy for me. As I read her books, I drew parallels to tidying up not just physical belongings, but in my relationships as well. I really started to focus on loving myself more, creating space to open up and truly become myself.

Relationships have always been difficult for me as I have struggled to connect authentically and fully with others because of my long hatred of myself. This season of tidying really allowed me to grow in loving who I am and lean into loving myself more than I ever have. I had to challenge some of the internal voices of hatred that had haunted me for so many years.

Another book that had a profound impact on my life at that point was "I Have Something to Tell You" by Chasten Buttigieg. I was substitute teaching when I discovered it, and it gave me courage and hope hearing his story and seeing that it was possible to make a difference and overcome the shame that had haunted me for so many years. I saw myself in his story and got inspired to share even more of my story with the world. I remember getting emotional several times while reading, to a point where I would have to stop a bit to regain my composure.

His story gave me hope that I could make a difference and be who I am simultaneously, something that I had thought was mutually exclusive for so many years. My initial attempt to attend college came out of a place of wanting to make a difference in the world. I wanted to become a youth pastor to help kids like me who had faced so many hardships and still managed to make life work for them. After my hopes of making a difference in that manner were dashed due to the rejection of my identity, I longed to find something that would give me an opportunity to change even just a small part of the world. I want to become the person I needed all those years ago and I can't wait to see that dream become a reality.

Shortly after my grandmother passed away, I started considering the thought of going back to school. I didn't know what it would look like and was not sure exactly how it would work, but it seemed doable. I started getting things together in September and applied to an online degree program with the local university.

During this same time, I was also substitute teaching. I had stumbled across it several months before when I was searching for a job. When I first started, it was just a job to get me through to something else. After a few months, it became something that I am extremely passionate about. I began to be requested by several districts and many teachers have my personal phone numbers to reach out when they need a substitute. The more I subbed, the more I knew that this could be something I was meant to do. I remember a long-term assignment that really impacted me. It was a week and a half assignment where I would be with the same class of students. At the beginning of the assignment, I was very unsure of myself because I was teaching the class and holding them accountable for their work. At the beginning, I had several students who would not listen to me, but by the end, they were turning in their assignments and doing so well.

    I saw myself in the students I served,

remembering the turbulent childhood that plagued my developing years. That assignment changed my life and I teared up on my last day with those students, knowing that I had made a small difference in their lives. I guess that is what I have been searching for for so long. I always tried to see a glimmer of making a difference in the world in other positions, but it was like I was grasping at straws with something that really was not making an impact. Substitute teaching was different though. When you leave the classroom for the day, you know for sure that you have made a difference in the lives of the students you serve.

Growing up, I had so many teachers encourage me and push me to do my best when I went home to a life of abuse and pain. I remember coming to school and seeing my teacher smile at me after being abused the night before. Their smiles and encouragement meant the world to me. I saw myself in the eyes of the students I served and always strived to encourage them and provide an atmosphere where they are supported in a way that will help them succeed.

My last year and a half of high school, I went from being very shy and quiet to a version of myself that I did not know was inside me. It was because of the wonderful teachers that I had that I regained confidence in myself and flourished. They may or may not have known what I was facing outside of school, but the difference they made in my life is unparalleled.

The other day, I stumbled across my

high school graduation speech that continues to inspire me to become who I was made to be and reclaim what life has tried to take away from me.

"As our future looms before us, we have to remember to make the most of every moment and embrace the future with unwavering optimism. Do not limit yourself to what you think you are capable of because chances are you are capable of so much more than that."

eleven

What I'm about to share with you is something I haven't told a lot of people in my life. It's been a difficult thing for me to accept personally, but I think it's also an important thing to share in the space of this book. In February of 2021, I tested positive for HIV-1. Up until this point, I hadn't had health insurance (or insurance that would cover anything at least) and went in to basically get tested for everything. I really didn't know what to expect as it had been so long since I had seen a doctor.

Growing up, healthcare was barely a priority and when something happened, we normally had to find a way to muscle through whatever ailment came up. I guess I carried this same thinking into my adult life, not knowing the importance of truly taking care of yourself. You hear it all the time when you're young. Adults will constantly say, "Take care of yourself!" in parting remarks, in letters, emails, etc. It's not until you begin your adult life that you finally realize what they meant. I remember being so anxious going into this doctor's appointment. For the year prior to this, I had had a few odd symptoms off and on and I was worried that it might've been something more serious than I let on. I won't go into detail here, but after a specific encounter with another man, there was pain that didn't go away with time and resulted in a rash that broke out over my body. I had just moved and thought that maybe the water in the new location had something in it that was making me break out so bad. I thought that maybe it was a cleaner I used. I didn't know what to do and after an ER visit with the symptoms, I still didn't have answers. I remember getting the call after the initial appointment with my PCP that something had come back abnormal, and they needed me to come back in for more tests. When I went back in, I remember bundling up, seeing my breath wisp in the air as I crossed the parking lot.

As I sat in the waiting room, I recall having a very real sense of how alone I felt. I hadn't told anyone about my experience and was worried about what could've been abnormal. I looked up at the big atrium that I sat in and wondered who my emergency contact would be if something was seriously wrong with me. Who would I tell? At this point, I had severed ties with the church I was attending (that I spoke about in my previous book), my Grandmother had passed away six short months earlier, and I was barely getting by. I felt completely alone and incredibly afraid.

    The office visit was short and only consisted of a visit to the lab to collect more blood. This time, they were testing for more specific things. By this point, I had access to the online portal where you can see results of tests, often before the doctor has the opportunity to tell you themselves. The day I got the news, I had received a notification on my phone that said new test results were available to view. I went over to my computer and logged in. I remember scanning all the results and looking for the bolded ones that I hadn't viewed yet. Then, there it was:

HIV-1 Test…..Expected Result: Negative….. Sample Result: Positive.

    The first emotion that I experienced in that moment was an encapsulating fear, knowing that I couldn't tell anyone around me. The first and only person I told was the guy I knew from Kansas City that was also the first person I came out to. In that moment, he provided a sense of stability in sharing with me that he too was HIV positive and that it gets better and that it's not a death sentence like it had been just a few decades earlier. That there's medication you take everyday that decrease your viral load and extend your life expectancy to that of a normal healthy person.

I remember thinking that I had done everything right. How was this possible? I had always worn condoms myself or had the other guy wear one. I had done everything right and somehow; I still got it. I wish I had known more, that I had educated myself more, not only about sex in general, but how to practice safe sex in the gay community. Up to that point, I hadn't been super sexually active, just the occasional hookup for fun. It was few and far between and I was inexperienced to say the least. I had grown up in such a sheltered environment that frowned on everything surrounding sex, demonized it, and made it this mysterious thing that not even adults are supposed to think about. It was such a taboo subject, that my only education had been what I had discovered in gay porn. I was so scared of it that, at that time, I was even scared to purchase lube off the internet, scared that someone would find out that I masturbate.

There I was, staring at the screen, trying to figure out what to do next. I couldn't stop looking at the result.

HIV-1.......Positive

It was so nonchalant. Like the result on the page didn't just change my life forever. It was such a cold presentation of data that has the potential to wreck the entire foundation of who you are. Then the phone call from my PCP came. She was the sweetest lady and sat with me in the news, allowing me to process and cry through it. I was a mess on the phone and she was so gracious and patient and sat with me in it. It rocked my world for sure and it shook the very foundation of who I am.

After my HIV diagnosis, suddenly a new closet appeared that grabbed at my identity and forced me to consider my existence in a brand new, more urgent light. This new closet felt a lot less comfortable than the one I had known before, a void that attempted to strike my identity with a fatal blow. I refused to believe the stigma perpetuated by the silence of my community and leaned in to believing in myself in a way I had never experienced before. My diagnosis was a new catalyst that was now pushing me toward the success I had always dreamed of. Still, navigating relationships under the cloud of my status was a weight I was ill-prepared to carry. Disclosing too early would result in limited or no connection at all. Disclosing too late would result in a broken heart and further isolation from a community I so desperately needed love and support from. Disclosing at just the right time was impossible to pinpoint. This closet was a closet I had to dismantle within myself to find the courage and strength to truly thrive.

    Oof, I can feel the tension you might be experiencing at this very moment. It's a lot to process. How could this published author, college student, activist; how could this successful person have HIV? Sometimes I ask myself the same question. It's been a lot to wrap my own head around and there are times that I wake up and don't quite believe it's true.

    I can't begin to describe to you the fear that I've experienced surrounding my diagnosis. Even in the LGBTQIA+ community, there's such a stigma surrounding it that pushes so many of us into a corner of isolation. As if we weren't already marginalized enough, my diagnosis felt like yet another marginalization of my existence. I felt, and sometimes still feel, so alone in it. I'm thankful for the friend I had in Kansas City that helped me to lean into accepting it more and destigmatize it a bit for myself. Sometimes it still feels like a cage that I want so desperately to get out of, but I'm scared of what might happen if I break the lock. With this book, I'm breaking the lock and owning my full identity as an HIV-positive gay man.

The months after my diagnosis were met with a lot of fear surrounding sex. I even found it quite difficult to masturbate because I couldn't stop thinking about it. There were several healthcare providers that were so gracious and kind throughout the process of diagnosis that helped me discover that this wasn't a life sentence, but a minor diagnosis that was treatable and manageable.

Still, I have the stigma of my illness in the back of my mind as I approach every interaction with others. I am cautious with friendships and have a bit of a process to ensure people that I allow into my life are decent human beings that won't treat me differently because of my illness. I also make it a point to share my status to new groups of people as I think talking about it works to further dismantle the stigma that still invades the topic of my illness.

With modern medicine, HIV is more manageable than diabetes. I take one pill a day in the evening, wake up in the morning, and go about my daily routine. When I first started treatment, I was a bit lethargic as I am a small guy and the effect the illness and medication had on my body was noticeable. Now that I've been on antiretrovirals for several years, it's a barely noticeable part of my life.

twelve

While my initial reaction to my diagnosis was one of dismay and disappointment, it quickly morphed into a catalyst that led me to some of the success I am now experiencing. My diagnosis was an amplifier of the ticking clock that hovers over all of our lives, a constant reminder that life is short and that you must do something with the time you're given. Up until that point, I had carried a lot of guilt about dropping out of college and wondered if the opportunity to try again would come. After COVID-19 hit and they entire world was collectively faced with their own mortality, this mirror of my mortal self catapulted me into fighting for myself so fervently that I became a version of myself unrecognizable to previous versions. It was like my life just downloaded a software update that sped up my performance and began fighting anything standing in my way. I remember jumping through all the hoops for my application for admission to Arkansas State University. From requesting my previous transcripts to preparing for the Accuplacer Exam, an exam adjacent to the ACT that would place me into the general education courses that would allow me to be the most successful. I spent countless hours at Panera with my coffee/charged lemonades studying for the exam. I retaught myself algebra, basic science, reading comprehension, and writing essentials, all from online materials and practice tests to prepare for the exam. The exam was only offered at a location about thirty minutes from my apartment. I remember using my last $12 to pay for the exam fee, eating ramen that entire week afterward. What started out as an Associate's in General Studies became three degrees that I now proudly hang over my desk in my home office. My Bachelor's in Business Administration, Associate's in Information Systems and Business Analytics, and a Certificate in Business Law and Compliance now serve me well as I work for a local non-profit organization that specializes in caring for people who have been through almost precisely what I've experienced.

  At A-State, I found community,

friendship, and rediscovered my love for music through the A-State Choirs and voice lessons with several incredible instructors. I became involved in a music fraternity and served as both Historian and Fraternity Education Officer for multiple years. My experience at A-State was one of redemption and rediscovery of my abilities, worth, and confidence after a long time of fruitless pursuits. I'm so thankful for the opportunity A-State provided me and the connections I made there and still have today. I attribute a lot of the success I'm seeing now to the care and consideration I was offered during my time there.

    I never thought I would find who I was meant to be. I had witnessed so many others find their way in life and be secretly jealous of the success they were experiencing. I have learned that when you find what you were meant to do, it's like breathing. You can do it in your sleep, and you wake up every morning, excited to do it all over again. I think I have found that. For a lot of people, it is a long journey of trying different things and hoping something sticks. I have experienced this and it's so hard to enjoy life when your job sucks the life out of you. When you are certain that you are making a difference, it doesn't matter how much money you make or where you live. You have found your calling, and it is indescribable.

I have talked a lot about my journey to where I am now in hopes that you might see yourself in it. For me, it has not been a straight line from high school to college to a successful career. I am still a work in progress. In many places, the cards were stacked against me in finding success. I tried to play them well, but I would always lose.

Once I finally accepted who I am inside, it allowed me to realize that I had the option to burn the cards that were stacked against me. It allowed me to open myself up to a life that brings me happiness and joy. If you are going through it right now as I was (and in many ways, still am), do not give up. Especially if you are part of the LGBTQIA+ community, do not give in to the hate that continues to be perpetuated by so many. You are valuable, you are worthy, and you are deserving of every dream that you aspire to obtain. Do not for a second think that you are inferior. I did for so long and it held me back and made me hate myself. Do not give anyone permission to discriminate against you. You are beautiful and loved. For me, it took walking away from the church for me to discover my self-worth. It took walking away from all of it to discover my true self and the life I genuinely deserved.

thirteen

Allow me to give us a bit of space to just breathe for a second. Breathe with me.

In.

...

...

Out.

...

...

In.

...

...

Out.

What we've just experienced together is heavy. I've shared my entire story with you and I know it's a lot to take in. There were boring parts, exciting parts, and horrible experiences of trauma that might have been difficult for you to read about. If you've found yourself relating to my story in any of these experiences, I am so sorry. What I've learned from talking to people who stop by my booth during my book tours is that my story is not an uncommon one. There are countless people who have similar life experiences that no one wants to talk about. People don't often want to talk about their experience leaving home because of their sexuality. People don't often want to talk about their experience with an HIV diagnosis. However, it's the silence that plunges us further into isolation. The goal of this book is to spark a conversation, allow us to speak up and share our stories so we can collectively know we are not alone.

In many ways, my HIV diagnosis was the catalyst that taught me to fight and fight hard for the life I wanted. It drove me to go back to school, complete my degrees, sing again, and truly find spaces where I can thrive.

Walking forward from trauma can mean a lot of things to different people. For some, walking forward is easy, second nature. For others, just getting up from a crawl can seem like a daunting task. For me, it has been a mixture of both trying to scrape by and find who I am all at the same time. Your past can sometimes sneak up behind you and pull you backward. Mine has several times. As I walk forward into the next chapter of my life, my hope is that I can put my turbulent past behind me, remembering the lessons I have learned, but not letting the tragic and sometimes painful experiences ruin the good things I have going on in my life. I've finally arrived at a place in my life where I feel as though I am fulfilling my calling, purpose, or whatever you like to call it. If you're in a similar place of trying to find yourself, don't lose heart. You deserve to become what you aspire to be, no matter what that dream looks like.

For so long, the hatred I had for myself held me hostage to a minimal life of limited connection and very few friends. I was always so hard on myself and would become defeated very easily. This manifested itself not only in my personal life, but in my professional life as well. The fear that I experienced when attending work, scared that someone would find out who I really was, filled me with anxiety. It led me to have noticeably short track records at various positions, often out of fear of being treated differently because of my sexual orientation.

Now, I still have a bit of that fear in the back of my mind as I move forward into loving myself more and becoming the most authentic version of myself that I can. Members of the LGBTQIA+ community should not have to endure this pain and fear of losing their livelihood simply for being who they are. We are not aliens, we are simply people that are looking for the same things you are in life. Love, happiness, and building a life that we are proud of are dreams that every human being has.

We all deserve to pursue happiness in life without the condemnation and criticism of institutions. We live in a country founded on these principals and have ventured so far away from providing this environment for so many. We need to build the capacity to open our hearts and minds to what love and the pursuit of happiness could look like for those in the LGBTQIA+ community without demonization and condemnation from so many hate-filled voices. When we have the courage to strike this balance, our world will truly be a better place for all of us.

I am a firm believer that the story of your life truly matters. It matters what you have been through. You can give hope and encouragement to others through your story by helping them realize that they are not alone. I have felt alone at many points in my life, but it has been through sharing my story that I have felt known and fully embraced to be the person I am becoming. I have always strived to be an encourager, simply because of the pain that I have endured. Even in your deepest pain, someone can find themselves in your story, discover a pivot point, and propel themselves forward into a life they are proud to live.

Within the LGBTQIA+ community, it is sometimes difficult to find authentic connection because of the pain that we have experienced. We have been pushed down and trampled on by so many, but I believe that through the power of our stories, we can change the perspective of many into one of love and understanding that might afford us a seat at the table in every realm of society.

For me, I have walked away from the church to find love for myself, but perhaps one day, the thought of returning will come, but not without setting clear boundaries for what is helpful and what is hurtful to those who are a part of the LGBT community. I believe there is still good in the thought of a God, but for so many, it has morphed into a vehicle to perpetuate hate against people groups they do not agree with and make themselves feel better about who they are. There are a lot of things wrong with this picture, and maybe one day, these stories of hurt and pain will be heard by the church without judgement, but with a kind and loving perspective that carries them to believe that love is all we ever wanted for ourselves. Our dreams are like those in the heterosexual community in that we all want love, family, friends, and a life that truly makes us happy. That is all we have ever wanted, and we deserve to find that.

For so many years, this pervasive cloud of shame constantly hovered over everything I did. Every job I held, every hobby I pursued, and even every relationship I tried to maintain was strained by my own self-hatred. I already had trouble making and maintaining friends because, while everyone else was learning how to do this, I was trying to make new acquaintances at my fifth high school. The entire time, I hated who I was inside. I had known that I was homosexual since the age of ten but was so terrified that someone would find out. I kept acquaintances at a distance, not wanting to allow them to see who I really was. I hid behind my identity as a "super religious" person while I desperately wanted to be my true self.

As I look back on my past, sometimes I wish I could go back and shake myself, telling younger John that I don't have to change who I am to make others happy, to make God happy, and that I have the human right to be EXACTLY who I am without apology. Sometimes I look back and shake my head at the John that once was, all the religious stuff I believed, how naive I was, how fake I was with people, and how I hid who I was out of fear. Now, I'm hoping to help others that might see a part of themselves in my story and wrap them in encouragement and help them with the tools I used to move forward.

 About six months ago, toward the end of 2021, I made the decision to go to counseling. As much as I wanted to believe I had put everything behind me, I still had moments of weakness every once and awhile and would think about the family members who have hurt and alienated me.

 Though expensive, going to counseling was absolutely one of the best decisions I have ever made for myself. It was online through a telehealth service which made it super convenient and accessible. My therapist was a wonderful man of color who was also a part of the LGBTQIA+ community. He was so nice and helpful, and I remember just basically spilling everything in my first session with him. I went through most of my family trauma, the bullet points at least, and he held my story in a space of care and consideration. There was a moment when we addressed my relationship, or lack thereof, with my father. I remember talking to him about it and how it ended and finally coming to the realization that I never mourned the loss of my relationship with him. We had been so close before he got remarried and I missed those times with him.

    Trying my best to move forward, I just pushed it away, focused on my studies, and kept going. It wasn't until I was able to slow down and find some space to breathe that I was able to make that realization. I cried several times during therapy and finally felt all the emotions that I hadn't had the courage (or time) to feel or process before. I was in a state of survival and didn't have time to feel. I can say that the three months that I was in therapy were some of the most impactful times of my life. I acknowledged my past, fully accepted it, and began the process of truly walking forward toward healing.

There was something that my therapist said during one of my sessions that I have kept with me today. To explain this fully, I'd have to give a bit of back story. We were talking about my pseudo-adopted families and how I had a sense of guilt about living with them and not being able to repay them for everything that they did for me. I felt as if I owed them something because they weren't my "real" family. What he said next really made a huge impact on me. He said, "…those people chose to do that. They didn't do that out of obligation but chose to help you because they cared about you. Wouldn't you want someone to be a part of your life because they truly care instead of family who felt they had to do it out of obligation?" He went on to explain the difference between someone doing something out of obligation and doing something because they care. I expressed to him how exhausting it was to feel the need to try to prove to people that I'm worthy of being cared for. I had felt discarded and pushed away by my family and felt guilty that I had to have other people in my life to take their place. I felt like I was a burden. What he said next is one of the most powerful things I learned from the experience. He said, "…think of it like an island. You're chilling out on your very own island, and you get to choose who you let on your island. If your family is unsupportive, hateful, judgmental, and is unhealthy for you to be around, you don't let them on your island. If they hurt you, they don't deserve to be on your island! Now, think of the people who have come into your life that you know care about you. They may not be family, but they care and have invested time and energy into showing their care for you. You've allowed them into your life because they've shown that they care and want to be on your island, not purely out of obligation."

Through tears, I began to realize that I shouldn't feel guilty about supportive, non-family relationships; that it's healthy to have supportive people in your life that care about you and want to see you succeed. I guess, for so long, I had felt so guilty that my family wasn't doing the things they should do to help me and that I had to rely on others to be that for me.

Now, as I'm moving forward, I tend to attract people that care about me and want to see me succeed. I've found it easier to trust people and make friends. It's been a process for sure, but it gets easier with time. This has led me to a wonderful life I'm leaning in to love. I am leaning in to love myself more than I ever have before. Relationships have always been a challenge for me, but I am pushing myself to become more open and trusting of others. I have started my search for my future husband and cannot wait to find him. I find myself dreaming of a cute little house with a wide-open yard where dogs could run and possibly an adopted child could play. I look forward to building a life together with someone who genuinely loves me for who I am and sees all the wonderful parts of me that I have struggled to see in myself. I have always enjoyed interior design and cannot wait to have a place of my own to decorate with beautiful furniture and décor, a place to entertain my chosen family and friends.

fourteen

No one really likes going to the gym, myself included. I had tried to go on my own a few times before and I would eventually stop going because I either lost motivation, or got too busy to find time. To be honest, I have always struggled with what I looked like in the mirror. I'm skinny and have always had trouble filling out. Right before the beginning of 2022, I decided to make a change. I had a friend who needed a workout buddy so I decided to sign up and start going. My personal trainer started me on a simple full body workout routine and helped me find a regimen that would lend itself to real results. In the first month I started seeing results and actually started liking what I saw in the mirror. Not only was I improving physically, but my mental health also improved. When I was feeling depressed, I would (and still) hit the gym and get some endorphins going. I would leave feeling strong and invincible. The pre-workout might've had something to do with that, lol. This may sound like a plug from a pumped personal trainer (I am neither), but it has seriously helped in my physical and mental space.

  All this to say, taking care of your physical health is important. From someone who came from an upbringing that barely provided for basic needs, taking my physical health seriously has always been a challenge. There's a sense of survival that a lot of us experience that come from poor households. We just want to get by and not stop to consider what we are consuming and how we are providing self-care for ourselves.

There's another aspect of this that took me a long time to consider. We might not truly believe that we deserve to take care of ourselves. For me, I had a cloud of self-hatred that plagued everything that I did. The relationships I had, the friendships I tried to maintain, everything was shrouded in an air of negativity and hatred. This even led to less than wonderful eating habits, having to force myself to eat at times and other physical manifestations of self-hatred. If you're having some of these same thoughts, it's important to take them captive and remind yourself that you deserve the good things that you are doing for yourself, in all aspects of life.

Within the LGBTQIA+ community, we feel so much pressure from those around us. This pressure seems to imply that we not only don't deserve to be ourselves, but that we don't deserve the wonderful things our life on earth has the potential to offer. Love, friendship, prosperity, and true, unfiltered, unmasked happiness. You deserve all these things. (Read that again!) I deserve all these things, and I hope that at least one thing I say in this book will help you on the path toward believing in your worth.

At the time of this writing, I am just winding down a summer book tour with my second book, "Walking Forward". In it, I recount when my parents discovered I was gay and the abuse and later departure from home that occurred. On the tour, I traveled all over Arkansas and came face to face with parents that didn't know what to do, a grandma that just wanted to show her granddaughter that she still loves her and her new girlfriend, a dad that didn't want to lose a son who just came out to him, a mom who wanted to show her non-binary teenager that a different gender identity wouldn't get in the way of their weekly shopping trips, a couple that just wanted to support their teenager through their transition. I met teenagers that just wanted a bracelet that represented who they are. Kids that lit up when they FINALLY found something to help them come out to their parents. And yet there were others who were going through a difficult situation with their parents and a grandparent had stepped in. Or ones who had left home years earlier, finally finding success for themselves, like me.

These experiences will stay with me for the rest of my life and I hope to make even more of an impact on the perspectives and thoughts surrounding the LGBTQIA+ community by those outside of it and also working within our community to foster love, true connection, and a mutual consideration of one another, something that a lot of us currently lack or overlook. It's hard to find true connection in the LGBTQIA+ community perhaps because a lot of us have had to fight so hard to simply be ourselves, much less allow others into our lives. There's an air of surface level connection that seems to pervade and plague us, seldomly finding connection on a more meaningful level. This has to change and I hope to be a part of that change.

Once we've pushed through our trauma, embraced who we are as a person, and truly begin the process of loving ourselves, we can finally see what it might look like to love what we see in the mirror.

Try It: Stand in front of a mirror and look yourself in the eye for five minutes. Set a timer and don't stop until it goes off. While looking in the mirror, consider everything you are as a person.

At first, only the negative things you see might be apparent. Maybe your hair is messed up or you're not wearing your favorite shirt. Let all the negativities fade away and start to focus on the things you like about yourself. You can start with visual things, maybe you've hit the gym hard and are starting to see progress. After the physical things, though, start to think about other characteristics of you. Think of one kind thing you did for another human that day. Maybe you held the door for someone; maybe you were there for a longtime friend, maybe you threw a surprise party for a coworker who just got a promotion. Think of all the little differences you've had an opportunity to make in the world and remember that you are worthy of the love and acceptance you receive from others and that you deserve to be exactly who you are in this moment.

It's important to love what we see in the mirror every day. Not just for the visual appeal, but to be conscious of everything you are in this moment and everything you mean to those around you. This isn't meant to go straight to your head. It's about being fully present and fully aware of your value as a human being. It's when you see your full value that you can look yourself in the mirror and genuinely appreciate the person staring back at you. It's important to take that time of reflection and realize your worth.

As our pace of life continually advances with the help of technological innovation, social media, and a general pressure to do and be more, it's important to find space to be fully present and disconnect from the distractions around us. One way that I do this personally is finding a spot in nature, go there, and simply exist. There's a state park not too far from my apartment and I go there frequently. I tie up my little ten dollar hammock to a couple of trees that overlook the lake and just allow myself to relax and be fully present in that moment. Sometimes, I'll go on a hike and sometimes I'll just lay there for a bit and breathe in the fresh air, listen to the birds chirping, and clear my head of all the things that have been on my mind. It's important to give yourself space to do this. If you have a busy schedule, like mine, you might have to carve out time for self-reflection, but the sense of being centered and at peace is worth it.

It can be difficult to find these spaces of peace, especially for those of us in the LGBTQIA+ community. Everything that we do seems to be constantly under attack or observation. Our right to simply exist in a space is consistently questioned, considered, or pushed aside. I've witnessed this in many spaces over the course of my life. Many of us find ourselves standing in the middle of these spaces, not knowing what to do. At first, we might think that we can change the space around us, convince others that we belong in it and that our sexuality or gender identity doesn't disqualify us from occupying that space. But, after determined conversations, what seems like a court room style trial, we surrender our wall of protection and those disqualifications start to seep into every part of our being making us believe that we don't belong in that space. GET OUT! If there are spaces like these that continually rob you of your identity, your peace, and your sense of self, you don't have to stay there! It took me quite a long time to realize this, especially with my own family.

Family is a difficult word for a lot of us in the LGBTQIA+ community. For some of us it recalls the most vivid pictures of abuse, for others it reminds us that Thanksgiving is just around the corner and that we don't have anyone to spend it with. For even more, it reminds us of days spent being forced to be something we aren't just to make those around us happy. There's a lot of weight to the word family for those of us who've experienced trauma and it's important to see these experiences from an outside perspective. As someone who has experienced mind-boggling trauma myself, it wasn't until I started looking at my family as friends that I was able to see what had happened to me from this new perspective. I had to take account of what these people said and the actions they took to hurt me and ask myself that if this was anyone else in my life, a friend, a co-worker, a colleague, etc.; would I have the same reaction? When it's family that is harming us, we tend to give them more grace than we should because we feel like we're obligated to do so. We feel as if they have some sort of bounce protection on the account of your life. If they harm us, they'll make up for it because they're family. When abuse happens, we tend to rationalize it in our head saying that this is what normal families do, this is what is supposed to happen. We often don't have the capacity to see that the actions that are taken against us are harmful and would be unacceptable if done to us by any other person.

    Oof, I can feel the heaviness in my chest of what I'm writing. For some of you reading this, you might be realizing, perhaps for the first time, that you are in an abusive situation. For others, you might have just made the decision to leave a situation that is robbing you of peace and joy in your life. Regardless of what just happened, it's important to know that you deserve to be exactly who you are. You shouldn't have to apologize to anyone around you for the person you are at this very moment. You deserve to have people around you that like the version of you that you currently are, not the version they hope to manipulate you into being. Just you is enough and if your situation isn't allowing you to be that, the people around you don't deserve your presence.

    Finding your place in the world is important. Whether it's the career you've always wanted, the friend circle you've longed for, or just accepting yourself exactly as you are. There's power in knowing exactly who you are and feeling free to be exactly that. Sometimes I think back over the course of my life and remember the person I was in the closet. I look on those years with a bit of hesitation and wish I had leaned in to love who I am sooner. I spent over 10 years in the closet and I think about all the years I spent hating who I am and wanting to be, and striving to become, someone I certainly am not. Religion does that to people. If you aren't careful, you can find yourself buried in it, causing harm to people when you don't even realize it because you believe that that is what "God" would have you do.

As someone who has experienced quite a bit of trauma, it's easy to recognize the draw religion has for hurting people. Those with low self-esteem, with tired hearts, and worn-out intentions stumble over a religion that promises to provide everything they've ever wanted: hope, dreams, and a life with purpose. What most discover, however, is empty promises, manipulation, and a stolen story used to make money. At least, that's what happened to me.

Since I left home at fifteen, I continue to discover the importance of boundaries and having the courage to leave a situation that is draining your energy, your hope, and even more so, the importance of finding situations that do the opposite. I've ended relationships with family members, would be friends, and others because of this. It's crucial to take stock of the people around you and consider how you feel in their presence. Are they encouraging? Do they want what's best for you or do they just want something from you? Do they tear you down, or build you up?

There's a moment where you must decide to do what is best for yourself and not feel selfish about it. As a textbook people pleaser, I still struggle with this a bit. I will go above and beyond for those in my circle, bend over backwards, and still feel like it's not enough. In finding and doing things that grow you, you'll discover that the life that forms around you is one you might just be happy to live.

At first, these healthy choices and boundaries might feel like the wrong decision because people start to see your success and start their attempts to tear it down. I've experienced this from family, friends, and even random strangers on Grindr, lol. It seems in a world of less relationships and more userships, all we think about is how we can cut another person down or discount what they bring to the table. What if we started treating each other with grace and hold them in a space of love and encouragement? We might discover that our lives become a lot brighter when that happens.

fifteen

Activism is incredibly important as an LGBTQIA+ individual. As a community, we are constantly attacked with injustice, discriminatory legislation, anti-gay rhetoric, and a myriad of other atrocities. It's only by standing up for yourself and others within your local community that you can truly find your voice and in doing so, inspire others to do the same. I've had the wonderful opportunity to do this just a handful of times and the impact it's made on my heart is something I don't take for granted. Get involved in your local community and do whatever you can, within the limits of your schedule, to help foster a space of positivity, love, support, and acceptance of each other so we can all feel safe, having a sense of togetherness and concern for one another. This is something that can easily be overlooked as we can have a tendency to tear each other down. We must reject that tendency to truly build a community others feel safe in and want to be a part of.

    The speeches that are in the attached appendix represent a time of incredible empowerment for me. They were as impactful for my own self-confidence as they were to fight against censorship and discrimination against the LGBTQIA+ community. I tend to try to project an image of confidence and self-assurance, but if I'm honest, I have a lot of moments where I feel less confident and sure of myself. I'm sure we all do, and that's completely okay. Don't be afraid to own that too.

Throughout my life, I've started over, time and time again. I've held various positions in various fields, just trying to find something that fits. What I've learned from these experiences is that you can't be afraid to do something new or pick up something again that you once held dear.

A big moment of pushing past this kind of fear was when I started the process of going back to school. I had been out of school for roughly seven years and had no clue if I could truly handle getting back to it.

I had experienced what it was like working full time in the workforce without a degree and found the experience to be underwhelming. You work incredibly hard, but no one recognizes your worth until you have a degree to back it up. I found it impossible to move up without a piece of paper showing that I know what I'm doing. It was frustrating to say the least, but I'm thankful for the experience because it allowed me to discover the true value of education.

  I've heard it said that you can do anything you put your mind to. It's a cliché phrase for sure, but I've found it to be true! I've put my mind to every job I've had, every position I've held, and have seen success in each one. I'm discovering that this is why I've had such a hard time finding what I want to do with my life because I can see what it would look like to be successful in a position and do just that.

If you come from a family that has not had the opportunity to pursue higher education for whatever reason, and are the first one going after a degree, you might be experiencing what I am. I tend to have constant feelings that I'm not good enough or smart enough to be doing what I'm doing. Those thoughts are contrasted by thoughts of pride in that I am the first in my immediate family to obtain a bachelor's degree. On my way to the bachelor's degree, I tied my father with his Associate's Degree education. There's no doubt that the day of graduation was an emotional one as I've fought really hard to have this incredible opportunity to pursue my education again and I'm incredibly grateful for everyone who has worked to help make it happen.

Don't let any of those thoughts that you're not good enough, smart enough, or deserving enough weigh you down. You are breaking thresholds that have held so many people back and you just have to keep going. You'll find as you lean in and apply yourself that you really can do amazing, groundbreaking things!

When I started out on my own, I had next to no tools to manage my finances. I hadn't had many good role models to look up to in that regard, or if they were, I had no idea how they managed their money effectively. After realizing the importance of this, I devised a system that I used in early adulthood that I still use today. I called it my LIFE BOOK. It's a small half-page binder that has worksheets for your current bills, debt management, car maintenance records, and savings records and places to keep it all together. It was a centralized location where I could see when/where my money is coming in and where it's going. It really helped me visualize what I'm doing with my money and how I can better manage it. I, by no means, claim to know all there is to know and still struggle sometimes to manage my own finances effectively, but I think it might be a helpful tool for anyone who needs something to get started. I have now published a version of my original LifeBook because I thought it might be helpful for you if you're looking for a way to effectively manage your finances without all the fancy bells and whistles (distractions) other financial management systems might offer.

    My highest purpose in sharing my story

and experiences with you is that you might find something in it to help you along your own journey. When I was experiencing all that I did, I so desperately wanted to know that I wasn't alone in my experience and I hope that this book becomes an encouraging mirror, allowing those that read it to not feel so isolated in their experiences. I've talked about a lot of heavy subjects, things that we tend to gloss over or forget about, in hopes that we might become less afraid to talk about and address them. If we are truly a community as our name suggests, we need to have these conversations without stigma or judgement to truly create a safe and loving space for everyone. By publishing this book, I hope this is the beginning of having the hard conversations, the needed conversations we must have to create a community where everyone is able to be exactly who they are free of stigma or judgement. Whether your closet was painted rainbow or a life altering disease, no one belongs in a dark cage, afraid to come out.

Until we begin having these difficult conversations, I will keep chasing my dreams and trying to make a difference in the world. I know that there are people that need to hear my story, and I look forward to sharing it with anyone that would have the ears to hear it. Our stories matter and need to be shared, heard, and supported. Thank you for taking the time to listen to mine.

sixteen

The following is a collection of writings I've penned over the years. Everything from my original oratory that won two awards in my high school years to my first attempts at creative writing, to speeches I've given to fight against bigotry, hate, and discrimination at a local library. Public speaking has been part of my life in several little spurts and my hope is that, one day, it might become something I do more often.

Original Oratory entitled "Tune In" (written September 2013, Parkview Speech & Debate)

The version provided here is the rough draft that underwent several (needed) edits before I used it to earn two awards my senior year of high school. I wish I could find the edited version, but it must've gotten lost in one of the many moves that occurred thereafter.

The Berkshire Mall was swarmed with avid shoppers. 49-year old Cathey Marrero was among them. As she ambled through the mall, however, her quest for that perfect gift was interrupted when she took a header into a rather larger fountain. Luckily, all that was hurt was her pride, especially after the YouTube video went viral. The world watched as Ms. Marrero, so consumed with texting, rather than walking, ended up drenched in the middle of a mall.

Distractions come from every angle, whether it's at work, at school, or even driving down the road. Einstein had it right when he said, "It has become appallingly obvious that our technology has exceeded our humanity. So, how do we focus in a world tuned out of reality and tuned in to the television? First, we can discover how this obsession has evolved. Then, we can identify the enablers of our addiction, and finally, we can analyze how this fixation on diversion harms not only our relationships, but our quality of life. Maybe its time to put down the phone, turn off the TV, and tune in to the world around us.

Philosophers from Socrates to Emanuel Kant thought that distractions were harmful to society. Socrates even went as far as to blame a written language for this dilemma. Immanuel Kant took a different approach. He believed distraction is attention split in half. Thus, we have voluntary and involuntary diversion. Involuntary diversion is absent-

mindedness—you know, when you walk into a room and have no idea why you went in; or you set down those pesky car keys while unloading the groceries and forget where they landed. On the other hand, if a distraction is intentional, it is called dissipation – like when your hairdresser gets so carried away with the salon gossip that you lose your pride to the scissors; or when dinner burns because the latest episode of Dr. Who just dropped on Netflix and needless to say, you were in the zone.

So, how did this cycle of distraction start? Cathy N. Davison, author of "Now You See It," explains that even as early as the Classical Era, distraction was worrisome. She outlines how Socrates proposed that a written language diminishes the mind, distracts us with an excess of information, contorts the power of memory, and oversimplifies the development of ideas that surface in dialogue. When Gutenberg developed a way to mass produce a written language, many feared that this overload of information would ahrm the human mind and once again oversimplify human interaction. Fast forward to today: cell phone, iPads, satellite dishes with hundreds of channels, and the likes of Facebook and Twitter put information—some useful, some not—at our fingertips. Now I doubt that the written word and the printing press are really to blame for the current state of affairs, but what is?

To cure this addiction we need to identify where it's coming from. Researcher, Daniel Gilbert, discovered that our minds wander 47% of the time. But why? The Social Times argues that the pace of modern life—spurred on by the technology that defines it—has reduced the average attention space from 12 minutes…to five in the past 10 years. Three major technological advances are among the enablers of this fixation on diversion.

First, Smart phones. We all have them and we all love them. Our relationship with our technology is almost as important as our relationship with our special someone. We have the world in our grasp and we just can't set it down…for a minute…gosh I wish I could check my phone right now. An uncontrollable addiction or a genuine way to communicate? The smart phone has become an enable of distraction that's ordered to-go. We check our phones up to 150 times a day. And we don't know when to stop. It's one thing to fall into a fountain because you have to send that text. It's another to take a life. According to Texting and Driving Statistics, 11 teenagers die a day in car accidents that involved texting.

  Television, TV, The Box. Everyone is a fan of one TV show or another, whether it's Duck Dynasty, Big Bang Theory, or Dr. Who, but what exactly do we gain from sitting in front of the television for hours on end? According to Nielsen Statistics, the average American over the age of two spends more than 34 hours a week watching television. The Bureau of Labor Statistics reports that 54 percent of children, when asked if they would rather watch TV *or spend time with their father, chose television. We've created a society where we fancy the remote more than our family.*

Finally, Social Media. More people around the world are "connected" than ever before, but are we really connecting or are we falling captive to another enabler of our addiction? Does our friend list on Facebook really show how many true friends we have? From Instagram and Pinterest to Snapchat, it's hard to tell the difference between quantity and quality when it comes to relationships. A recent study by the Huffington Post revealed that the average Facebook user has 130 friends. Obtaining friends has never been easier, or has it. This distraction of collecting friends and "connecting" with people has obliterated the true definition of a relationship. Accodring to social media examiner, when it comes to relationships "We run the risk of alienating the people who populate our daily lives in pursuit of intimacy with our online friends." As technology evolves faster and faster every day, we have to stop and realize how this overload of information is taking a toll on not only our relationships but our lives.

The Washington Post tells the story of Miles Harrison, a devout husband and father. Drenched in private torment and emotional trauma, his feeling of remorse was as powerful as an addiction, except this time, there was no cure. One torid day in July, Miles was going about his daily routine of making phone call after phone call on his way to work. In his stupor, Miles forgot to drop-off his son, Chase at day care. "The toddler slowly sweltered to death, strapped into a car seat for nearly nine hours, in an office parking lot in the blistering heat of July.

The question is what can we do to break this addiction. How can we focus so that future generations don't follow in our dangerous footsteps? John Lennon wisely describe the distracted culture that we inhabit today when he sang, "Life is what happens to you while you're busy making other plans." When we stop doing a million things at once and start appreciating the life that we have and the precious gifts of family and friends, we begin to revoer from our addiction. We have to guard our minds against the pace of life and allow ourselves to give what matters our full attention. Psychologist Mathew Killingworth actually found that happiness is greater when our thoughts are focused. We will begin to open up and smile a little more. Allow yourself to break away from distraction and turn to purpose: ignore that incoming email, read an actual book, even play Monopoly with your family instead of texting each other when dinner is ready.

    Socrates was right to be afraid of distractions. So maybe you haven't took an unexpected swim in the middle of a mall. But we can all admit to being distracted at some point, whether it's planning your weekend while in that meeting with your boss, checking the latest status update of your 300 besties, or playing Words with Friends while your daughter asks you for help with her homework. And really, that's a shame. We need to focus on the things that matter. Life isn't about how many "followers" we have; it's how many true relationships that we earn. Maybe it's time we put down the phone, turn off the TV, and tune in to the world, the people, around us.

Library Speech #1: Given August 14th, 2021 at Craighead County Jonesboro Public Library Board Meeting

"Love is patient and kind. Love is not jealous or boastful or proud or rude. It does not demand its own way. It is not irritable, and it keeps no record of being wronged. It does not rejoice about injustice but rejoices whenever the truth wins out. Love never gives up, never loses faith, is always hopeful, and endures through every circumstance." 1 Corinthians 13: 4-7 Like many of you in this room, I grew up in the church. I was also taught the Golden Rule in Sunday

school. "Do unto others as you would have them do unto you." Matthew 7:12. I quickly learned, however, that this was just a phrase, just a string of words Christians like to throw around to cover up discrimination and manipulation.

When I was ten, my parents got divorced and I later learned that my mother left my father for a woman. I was terrified because the messages that I would hear from Sunday school teachers and pastors was that gay people were going to hell and were not deserving of anything good in this life, that they were vile human beings and not deserving of human decency or respect. The pastor constantly found opportunities to demonize the LGBT community and made them out to be something less than human. The church even went so far as to print off a list of companies that supported the LGBT community and told us that if we bought anything from these companies that we were sinning and going to hell.

We kept attending church, but relationships and

connections disappeared quickly as news spread about my mom. It was in the following years that I started to develop my own same sex attraction. This compounded my fear and led me to fabricate a façade of holiness that I would carry into the teenage and early adult years of my life. As my pre-teen years went on, I continued to hide this from my father out of fear of what might happen if he found out. My hiding tactics didn't last too long as he discovered pictures of attractive shirtless men on my iPod touch I had saved up to buy.

I remember that night like it was yesterday. I was in my room and my father came upstairs to let me know that dinner was ready and caught me looking at the pictures on my iPod. He snatched it away from me and gave me a look of eternal hatred before he rushed downstairs to talk with my stepmom. After an intense few hour of interrogation, my father made me watch as he took a hammer to the iPod touch I had bought. After smashing it to bits, he placed it in a

Ziplock bag and hung it over the kitchen sink to remind me, every time I did my daily chores, how much they hated me. The abuse got worse and worse as I was forced to do every chore in the house and was beaten until I couldn't sit or lay down if they found one speck of dust on something that I cleaned.
They slowly took away everything away from me that brought me joy. Books, movies, video games, and even fun school projects were taken away from me. I had a knack for music and I was forbidden to practice inside the house and my alto saxophone was eventually sold so they could buy fun things for my step-siblings. I lived in a hell that God created as my father and stepmother believed that they were doing what God would have them do. The beatings came to a head after my stepmother got into an argument with my father over me and forced me to sleep on a mattress in their master bedroom while she slept in my bed. After fighting until the wee hours of the morning, my stepmother tried to wake me up at 7am and I

physically couldn't get up out of physical and emotional exhaustion. She then proceeded to flip the mattress and throw me across the room, my head slamming into the computer desk behind me. She then held me down and slapped me until my face turned dark red and her hand got tired.

I finally mustered the courage to leave home on foot when I was fifteen. It was a chilly April evening and after finding a few flecks of dust under a pile of dirty laundry that I had swept around, my stepmom lost it and started yelling obscenities at me. She told me to go for a walk and I did. Walking on the side of the road, I desperately wanted to believe that there was a God that loved me and at the time, I still did. I hated myself so much that I thought that if only I could be holy enough that God would love me enough to fix me. He hasn't and he won't because I now know that there is nothing wrong with who I am. I don't have to fit within the circus act of a religion to know that there is a God who loves me and cares for each one of us,

regardless of our identity or sexual orientation.
My experience is not uncommon. There are countless stories of homeless LGBTQ youth who have left or been kicked out of their homes at a young age for simply being who they are. There are kids that have contemplated or ultimately committed suicide because of their fight against their identity or attraction and the voices of hate that continue to be perpetuated by many of you in this room. Look down. Their blood is on your hands and it's not coming off.
If I would've walked in to our public library all those years ago and saw a display the celebrated who I am and refused to perpetuate hate and discrimination against a lifestyle different than our bigoted conservative Christian community, I would've known that the abuse that I was experiencing was not okay. The abuse I endured did not come from a God who loved me, but from a religion that continues to manipulate and torment people under the guise of love. I would've known that I am not alone. I would've

known that I am worthy of love, acceptance, friends, family, and everything that I aspire to be. I would've known that there is nothing wrong with the life that I will have with my future husband.

The truth is that our dreams are like those in the heterosexual community in that we all want love, acceptance, and a life that truly makes us happy. We deserve to find that without harmful bigotry and abuse from churches that monetize manipulation. I dream of a world where we can live simultaneously together and hold each other in the highest regard, regardless of our identity or sexual orientation. I dream of a world where this argument that we are having today would make us laugh at ourselves and dismiss it as insanity. I dream of a world where love is love and we are all the better for it. Thank you.

Library Speech #2: Given January 2nd,

2022 at Craighead County Jonesboro Public Library Board Meeting

"Seriously they want me to wear purple because five queers killed themselves. The only way I'm wearing it for them is if they all commit suicide. I can't believe the people of this world have gotten this stupid. We are honoring the fact that they sinned and killed themselves because of their sin. REALLY PEOPLE?"

"I would disown my kids if they were gay. They will not be welcome at my home or in my vicinity. I will absolutely run them off. Of course, my kids will know better. My kids will have solid Christian beliefs. See, it infects everyone."

Those were the words of a School Board Member at Midland School District near Floral, Arkansas, 90 minutes from that door. He was vocal on social media about wearing purple in support of the LGBTQIA+ community after five queer students committed suicide in the school district.

It breaks my heart thinking about these stories, knowing that I have experienced some of the same ignorance, the same refusal to understand among my own family. When I left home at fifteen, I had some of those same words internalized, constantly thinking that something was seriously wrong with me because I'm gay. "It's a sin!" "You're going to hell!" "You should just kill yourself!" I would try so hard not to think about it, thinking that somehow, I did something to make myself gay. Over the passed few months we've heard from so many in our community. We've witnessed this kind of hatred firsthand from former library board members, pastors, teachers, and others that are shaping the minds of our next generation.

What kind of children are you raising? Are you raising children that understand that it's okay to be different, and for others to be different, or are you raising kids that bully others because they don't fit the mold you want to put them in? Are you raising children that sit with the outcast at lunch, or play four-square with the gay kid at recess? Or are you raising children that torment the gay kid and make them feel like they belong in the trash? Are you raising children that think it's perfectly okay to drag a library board, staff, and directors through the dirt for 6 months, bringing harm to their mental, emotional, and possibly physical health and that of their families and loved ones? Are you raising children that file lawsuits against a library board because they can't bear the thought of including material in a public collection that might be helpful for someone they refuse to understand? Are you raising children that know that it's not okay to treat someone differently based on their socio-economic status, race, religion, ethnicity, and yes, sexual orientation or identity? That's what this is about. Are we raising better human beings than ourselves? Are we teaching them, and setting a good example of, how to be a good human being and how to love people that might happen to be different than us? From what some have shown in this beautiful new addition to the Children's Library, my answer is no. What others have taught the children watching us in this community is that it's not okay to be different. That it's not okay to express yourself and be exactly who you are. That it's perfectly okay to grow into adult bullies that continue to minimize and diminish the identity of the LGBTQIA+ community simply because it's something they are afraid of and refuse to comprehend. I can't bear the thought of what might happen if some of these same hateful people had a child that came out to them. The abuse that happens behind closed doors, the alienation from their own parents, and the eventual departure from home. We are tired of it. We are tired of seeing suicides in our own communities, tired of hearing about school board members endorsing and perpetuating hate speech against innocent minors, telling them that they should kill themselves. We are tired of hearing pastors joke about PRIDE, making us out to be terrible, indecent human beings. IT STOPS RIGHT HERE. Our libraries are a place that allow us to learn about people that are different than us. Our libraries are sacred spaces that offer information to all without bias. This isn't a church library, a Sunday school bookshelf. If you want one of those, go back to your church. This is a PUBLIC LIBRARY where all viewpoints, perspectives, and social groups should be represented without question or rebuttal. We refuse to be diminished and pushed aside by hate filled, ignorant pastors, childcare workers, teachers, and others that continue to be the cause of suicide among our community. We won't stand for this, and we will keep fighting until it stops. Their blood is still on your hands, and it won't come off.

Our stories are important. Our stories are not inappropriate. Our stories are vital to saving the lives of young people who are grappling with their sexuality in a world that perpetuates hate and discrimination against them. Our stories have the power to change people's minds about the LGBTQIA+ community and that is the sole reason why these books are being challenged. They are grasping at straws that are slipping away because people's minds are changing. People are waking up to thinly veiled hatred, walking away from churches that perpetuate blatant discrimination. We will not stop fighting for our community, for ourselves, and for the protection of the LGBTQIA+ community in all spaces. I continue to dream of a world where love is love and we are all the better for it and we won't stop fighting until that happens.

Speech #3: Given September 12, 2022 at Craighead County Jonesboro Public

Library

"I'm telling you, if I had any mental issues, they would all be plowed down with a freaking gun by now." Those were the words of Melissa Bosch during a Mom's For Liberty meeting this summer in Cabot, Arkansas, referring to librarians and her anger about LGBTQIA+ material being available in a school library. According to the Los Angeles Blade, Ms. Bosch and the Mom's For Liberty Group she's apart of advocates for [banning](#) "pornographic books" to protect children, parroting a line right-wing media often use to [target books](#) about race, sexuality, and LGBTQIA+ identity. Sound familiar?

If you're in this room right now, you're no stranger to that kind of toxic rhetoric. You've heard countless Mom's For Liberty puppets get up here and talk so fervently about how they're trying to protect children. They've called gay men like me pedophiles, groomers, vagrants, and other names I'd rather not repeat. What they fail to see is that we're trying to protect children too, from toxic parents like them.

I recently completed a summer book tour with my book, "Walking Forward". In it, I recount when my parents discovered I was gay and the abuse and later departure from home that occurred. On the tour, I traveled all over Arkansas and came face to face with parents that didn't know what to do, a grandma that just wanted to show her granddaughter that she still loves her and her new girlfriend, a dad that didn't want to lose a son who just came out to him, a mom who wanted to show her non-binary teenager that a different gender identity wouldn't get in the way of their weekly shopping trips, a couple that just wanted to support their teenager through transition. I met teenagers that just wanted a bracelet that represented who they are. Kids that lit up when they FINALLY found something to help them come out to their *parents. And yet there were others who were going through a difficult situation with their parents and a grandparent had stepped in. Or ones who had left home years earlier, finally finding success for themselves, like me.*

These experiences had a profound impact on me, reminding me that we truly are the ones protecting children. I think there was a prepositional phrase left out of the Mom's for Liberty "protecting children" rhetoric. These fanatics are all about protecting children "from becoming a part of the LGBTQIA+ community". Make no mistake, that is all they are concerned about because they are afraid that they will have a child that eventually comes out to them and they won't know what to do. What keeps me up at night is what some of these extremist, toxic parents might do to their children if that happens.

There are many of you on this board that can't see

past your hatred of the LGBTQIA+ community to realize what you're doing. I get it, I've been there, I understand what your religion is making you do. But there's a point where you must step back and realize that the people you're trying to demonize are some of the same people that once sat in your pews. They're the same people that once believed in the God you use to shame us, ridicule us, judge us, and ultimately reject us.

I don't get up here just to relive my past trauma. Trust me, it's not fun. The reason I get up here is that I know that there are so many more John Caldwell's out there that don't feel like they have a voice because of you. They're scared to call out shitty, toxic behavior when they see it and are afraid to use their voice to effect change in their communities. I assure you; we will not be silent as we continue our fight to protect LGBTQIA+ youth in our community and throughout Arkansas. We're here, we're queer, we're not going away, and we deserve a spot on that shelf! Thank you.

Research Project for Composition II at Arkansas State University – Spring 2022

The following is a research project I completed for one of my classes early on in my college journey. Entitled, "The Dinner Table Dilemma: Responding to and Supporting Your LGBTQIA+ Teenager, I completed research into what LGBTQIA+ teenagers experience in the classroom, at home, and in society and the impact a positive coming out experience could have on them. I also explore how religion has the potential to harm those that come out with unneeded shame and ridicule facilitated by the church.

Introduction

"I'm Gay." Two words heard by parents at dinner tables across the nation. What happens in the

moments after this statement are crucial for the relationship between parents and LGBTQIA+ adolescents. Positive reactions can lead to healthy, flourishing relationships and reduce risk factors that are so often associated with the LGBTQIA+ community. Negative reactions, however, can cause self-hatred, self-harm, abuse, and might ultimately lead to the tragic suicide of your emerging adult. In this exploration of issues surrounding the LGBTQIA+ community, I plan to equip you with the tools you need to, at most, support and encourage your LGBTQIA+ adolescent, and at least, help you in becoming a needed ally. Through scholarly research and personal accounts, I hope to offer a detailed perspective of the atrocities LGBTQIA+ youth experience and how we can work together to change the mindsets and biases that cause them.

The Problem

As a gay man myself, I have experienced many of the same things I will talk about in my *research. My father discovered I was gay when I was roughly 13 years old. I was in my room, privately looking at pictures of shirtless men on an iPod touch I had saved up to buy. My father barged in without knocking, as he often did, making me jump and quickly lock my iPod. He then forced me to unlock it, revealing pictures of attractive shirtless men. With a shocked look of disgust, my father ran downstairs to talk with my stepmom. What felt like an eternity passed as I had a panic attack in my on-suite bathroom. I started hyperventilating and after a few minutes was able to bring myself together before my father called for me to come down and talk with them. An intense few-hour interrogation followed before my father made me watch as he took a hammer to the iPod Touch I had bought. After smashing it to bits, he put the pieces in a zip-lock bag and hung it over the kitchen sink to remind me every day how much they hated me.*

This was the beginning of continuous abuse I

endured from my father and stepmother. They used everything they could to punish me. Taking game systems away, selling my alto-saxophone, even taking books that I enjoyed reading away so that my existence was limited to the basic things one needs to survive: food, water, sleep, and shelter, not to mention an endless list of chores I had to complete each day. They made me into a shell of a human, not allowing me to even enjoy family movie nights together. Instead, I would have to scrub the kitchen floor with a rag while they watched "The Avengers".

While my experience may seem extreme, and it may be in some ways, I'm not alone in my experience. In a study conducted by The Journal of the American Medical Association, many high school students experience discrimination, stigma, and bullying in the adolescent years both at school and at home. These experiences can lead to students feeling worthless, having thoughts of suicide, and some even deciding to take their own life. In this study that took a broad sample of high schools across the United States, out of 9-12 grade LGB and questioning students, a staggering 549,980 of them have seriously considered suicide, 490,870 have made a suicide plan, and 120,790 students had a suicide attempt that resulted in an injury that required medical attention. It's clear that we have a glaring problem that needs urgent attention, discussion, and immediate actions taken to protect LGBTQIA+ adolescents.

Origins

Where do these conversations of discrimination toward the LGBTQIA+ community originate? Well, most of us have experienced it from the earliest stages of adolescence. As we are developing into adults in these early, emerging stages, we tend to experience a deep desire to be "normal". We want to be cool and fit in, and anything outside of that paradigm plunges us into social ruin that has the potential to shake our emotional, mental, and even physical lives.

In a study conducted by a university in the Midwest, several doctoral candidates of social work embarked on a journey to discover the impact the phrase, "That's so gay!" could have on the physical, emotional, and mental wellbeing of college students. The results concluded that the use of the phrase from heterosexual people among those apart of the LGB community had direct, negative correlations to specific health factors including their feeling of acceptance, self-esteem, anxiety, headaches, trouble eating, and comfort talking about their sexual orientation. Using this phrase in a negative, mocking manner, aligning being gay to an undesirable action or way of being truly has an impact on those of us in the LGBTQIA+ community.

Another source of negative thoughts and stereotypes surrounding those in the LGBTQIA+ community come from religious points of view. When conducting my research, a local educator reached out to offer a bit of perspective on this topic. "A large part of our community considers themselves Christian, and, as such, they use that as an excuse to hurl bigoted statements." Her sentiments give light to the profoundly tragic impact religion can have on perpetuating untrue and unfair accusations and opinions of the LGBTQIA+ community, giving a footing to the hatred so many have toward us. Religion can have a quite manipulative and persuasive way of getting people to think and act a certain way, making it difficult to reason and share empathy with those that are different than them. This rigidity can, in the most extreme cases, lend to hate crimes and tragic violence where those committing these acts feel "compelled by God" to do so.

What You Can Do

At the beginning of this research project, I posted on Facebook asking for input from parents, educators, allies, and others. While my initial post only garnered one response, after urging more to respond through posting it again with an emphatic plea for help, I received a few eye-opening responses. One local parent responded," As far as talking to my kid about LGBTQIA+, I'm not sure that she has the mental competence to understand it." When asked a follow-up question about what that conversation might look like when her child gets older and may be able to understand it a bit more, she responded: "I'm not entirely sure. Let me think about it and I'll get back to you." This knee-jerk reaction is not uncommon among parents both that are raising heterosexual children and parents that have an adolescent who has come out to them. Even in my own research, it was difficult to find solid scholarly research in this area, perhaps because so many are so afraid of it.

In a study published in The Family Journal *entitled* Family Support Would Have Been Like Amazing: LGBTQ Youth Experiences with Parental and Family Support, *Stuart Roe conducted ground-breaking research on what LGBTQIA+ youth experience within their homes and what support, or lack thereof looks like for adolescents who come out as part of the LGBTQIA+ community. From his research emerged four things you should know about what LGBTQIA+ youth experience.*

The first of these is that coming out is necessary. In a response from one of the students interviewed for the study, the necessity of coming out is revealed as a step in preserving his mental health. "Yeah, I had to, it was like really, really, really, really messing me up just hiding it every single day or putting effort into hiding it…it felt much better just to be myself." (Marco 57) His sentiments illustrate the immense pressure placed on those apart of the LGBTQIA+ community that have yet to come out of the closet and are still struggling to accept who they are. As a gay man myself, I've experienced this pervasive feeling that siphons your energy, physical and mental strength, and can even make you do extreme things to prove to others that you are not indeed gay. I remember in middle school, buying flowers, cards, and gifts for the most popular girls in school, simply because I wanted to prove to everyone that I wasn't gay.

The second thing Roe found during this study is that the initial response from parents is most often not a positive one. One tragic experience shared by Jonathan in his interview illustrates the sometimes-extreme rejection experienced by LGBTQIA+ youth. During a conversation talking about how his parents took him to court after coming out, Jonathan says "They wrote a letter disowning me and signing it at the bottom saying for homosexuality [and a host of other behaviors]." I honestly teared up when I first read that during my research. While I did not go as far as a courtroom when being disowned by my family, I did experience some of the same forms of hatred and rejection of my identity by family and friends. I can't imagine having that played out in front of strangers in a courtroom. These knee-jerk responses must stop and be replaced by more supportive, positive actions taken by parents, family, and friends.

As discussed briefly in an earlier section, Roe also found that LGBTQ youth view religion as a barrier to support from parents. During his research, he found that "Many of the students interviewed were previously involved in the churches attended by their parents, but as they became more aware of their sexuality, they decided not to attend." (Roe 57) One respondent detailed his experience when talking privately with leadership of the church he attended. Devin, one of the students interviewed during the study remembers his experience of dealing with church leadership regarding his sexuality. "Yeah, like what did they call it, you need to recant your ways or pray or something to fix it, and I was like, it is not something to be fixed and it is me, and eventually the church said, well if you are not going to even try to fix yourself then why come? And since then, I haven't gone." Devin went on to say, "I don't go to church anymore because, I don't think, I don't think I'd be accepted at

*the church I used to go, so I don't..., I don't know."
Devin's experience is not uncommon. I, myself, grew
up in a Christian household that took religion quite
seriously. I was even part of leadership in my youth
group as a worship leader, on the worship team, and
volunteered during the summer at my church. After
going off to a Christian college, I realized that my
religion and sexuality were incompatible. I eventually
left all of it behind in search of what being a good
human could look like outside of the confines of the
dogma of religious circles.*

  *The fourth and final finding of Roe's study
was that youth want explicit support and
encouragement from their parents, family, and friends.
He explains, "Improving relationships between
LGBTQ youth and their parents is important for the
health and well-being of LGBTQ youth, but very little
is known about how to improve that relationship."
(Roe 58). Throughout this research I've found that the
most important thing in this area is to avoid the knee-*

jerk reaction that so often occurs within family settings and offer an individualistic approach, urging the adolescent to pursue who they want to be, similar to the age-old adage of "Chase Your Dreams!". All we really want is support and empathy from our family and providing even the slighted affirmation of who we are can have profound implications for the success and well-being of your emerging adult.

Final Thoughts

Perhaps the most important take-away from this study is that LGBTQIA+ people need support from the earliest stages of accepting who they are. You have an incredible opportunity to step in and be that support they need at a critical time in their journey toward adulthood. This support can take many shapes and forms and may not even need to address their sexuality directly. When I was discovering this about myself in my developing stages of middle and high school, having supportive teachers, librarians, choir directors, coaches, and others helped me become more confident in who I am as a whole person including my sexuality. While it took me a bit more time to be completely solid in my identity as a gay man, I still remember the impacts, both positive and negative, others had on my experience. You now have at your disposal, a few powerful tools to make an enormous impact on someone you know who is a part of the LGBTQIA+ community, or might still be closeted, hoping to find someone like you to support and encourage them in their journey.

Resources

1) Hoffman, Marvin. "Teaching "Torch Song": Gay Literature in the Classroom." English Journal, vol. 82, no. 5, 1993, pp. 55-58.

2) Moita-Lopes, Luiz P. "Queering Literacy Teaching: Analyzing Gay- Themed Discourses in a Fifth-Grade Class in Brazil." Journal of Language, Identity, and Education, vol. 5, no. 1, 2006, pp. 31-50.

3) *Respondent #1 – Local Parent*
4) *Respondent #2 – Local Parent*
5) *Respondent #3 – Local Educator*
6) *Respondent #4 – Local Educator and member of LGBTQIA+ community*
*Identities of local respondents have been kept anonymous as to protect them from potential discrimination and retaliation from employers, family, friends, and others who might take discriminatory action against them. *
7) Roe, Stuart. "Family Support would have been Like Amazing: LGBTQ Youth Experiences with Parental and Family Support." The Family Journal (Alexandria, Va.), vol. 25, no. 1, 2017, pp. 55-62.
8) Woodford, Michael R., et al. ""that's so Gay!": Examining the Covariates of Hearing this Expression among Gay, Lesbian, and Bisexual College Students." Journal of American College Health, vol. 60, no. 6, 2012, pp. 429-434.

9) Zaza, Stephanie, Laura Kann, and Lisa C. Barrios. "Lesbian, Gay, and Bisexual Adolescents: Population Estimate and Prevalence of Health Behaviors." *JAMA : The Journal of the American Medical Association*, vol. 316, no. 22, 2016, pp. 2355-2356.

This research paper was an impactful experience for me as I had known my own experience during my childhood but did not yet grasp how common it was. It was both heartbreaking and inspiring in that it inspired me to do more and be more for my local LGBTQIA+ community.

Made in the USA
Coppell, TX
21 February 2026

71984220R10164